THE HISTORY
OF
AMERICA

THE HISTORY
OF
AMERICA

Robert A. Collins

SMITHMARK

Edited by
David Gibbon

Commissioning Editor
Andrew Preston

Designed by
Anthony Dominy

Photographic Research
Leora Kahn
Meredith Greenfield

Production
Ruth Arthur
Sally Connolly
Neil Randles

Director of Production
Gerald Hughes

This edition published in 1993 by SMITHMARK Publishers Inc., 16 East 32nd Street, New York, NY 10016.

SMITHMARK books are available for bulk purchase for sales promotion and premium use. For details write or call the manager of special sales, SMITHMARK Publishers Inc., 16 East 32nd Street, New York, NY 10016; (212) 532-6600.

CLB 2636

Produced by CLB Publishing Ltd., Godalming Business Center, Woolsack Way, Godalming, Surrey GU7 1XW, England.

ISBN 0-8317-4482-0

Printed and bound in Hong Kong.

10 9 8 7 6 5 4 3 2 1

Left: *In New York City in the 1920s, jazz was in the air and another glittering nightclub was always just a short taxicab ride away.*

CONTENTS

INTRODUCTION

In the scheme of things, America is a relative upstart. Long before Europeans began arriving on its shores, great civilizations had flourished and faded into obscurity; great empires had dominated the world and eventually died. The Italian Renaissance had produced such towering figures as Giotto and Leonardo, and the English had been living under the terms of the Magna Carta for almost three hundred years.

But the world took a dramatic turn on that day in 1492 when Christopher Columbus sailed into the Caribbean, and although naysayers have taken to downgrading his accomplishment, there is no denying he handed an unprecedented opportunity to all humankind to break patterns that had dominated the world for thousands of years.

Old ideas die hard, to be sure, and the American idea of creating a more perfect society is still evolving. But considering that the work has been in progress for less than five hundred years, the twinkling of an eye compared to the development of other cultures, the results have been fascinating.

The story so far is filled with rogues and rascals, and conspiracies real and imagined. But it is also laced with tales of men and women who came to America for a better life and not only found it, but bettered the lives of their neighbors as well as their fellow humans in other parts of the world.

When the former immigration center at New York's Ellis Island was reopened as a museum, millions of Americans began flocking there in search of their roots. But, significantly, the first immigrant to set foot on the island arrived there in 1892, when America was already well into its second century as a nation of immigrants. And through all of those years, each family that arrived brought something new to the creation of a new and different culture that, in the final analysis, is less the product of their adopted country's history than among people in other parts of the world whose common past is ingrained in their souls.

What we all share is the history of the American experience. It is the common thread that translates the determination of the Jamestown settlers into the will to succeed that is alive and well among the Korean immigrant families that dominate New York's fresh fruit and vegetable trade today. It is the stuff of dreams, especially the American Dream: the proposition that anybody who is willing to work can make something of themselves no matter where they came from, no matter what their family background.

Americans have had their share of heroes and more than a few antiheroes as well, but those among us whose primary goal is to be Number One in everything we do generally get their inspiration from ordinary people who challenged themselves to do extraordinary things. The Minutemen who stood their ground at Concord Bridge, the pioneers who opened the West, the men who put their lives on the line to help release Europe from the grip of two world wars, and all the others in between who gave what they could, and then some, make America the envy of a much older world.

Left: *The Statue of Liberty greets 19th century European immigrants to their new homeland.*

CARIBBEAN CRUISING

Facing page: Christopher Columbus, an Italian from Genoa, planted the flag of the King and Queen of Spain in the New World at the edge of the Caribbean Sea.

It wasn't the average Caribbean cruise, with disco dancing, midnight feasts and lounge chairs topside by the pool. But the itinerary of Christopher Columbus's explorations of what, thanks to him, became known as the Spanish Main would have modern Americans eagerly reaching for their checkbooks.

Columbus was a good promoter and a master map-maker, but it took him nearly ten years to sell the idea of history's first Caribbean cruise. He himself got the idea from a fellow Italian, Paolo Toscanelli, a Florentine who had studied the reports of the Venetian Marco Polo and made a map of the Far East that placed Japan some fifteen hundred miles off the coast of China. He also said that it wasn't very far from the west coast of Europe, exactly twenty four hundred miles in fact, and that the east could easily

be reached by sailing west. Christopher Columbus and his brother Bartholomew enthusiastically agreed and began a tour of the courts of Europe armed with their maps and their powers of salesmanship. They were politely received and just as politely put off everywhere they went, but doors weren't slammed in their faces. Queen Isabella and King Ferdinand of Spain had turned the proposal over to a committee, and King John II of Portugal asked for time to think it over. The Portuguese were first to give the Columbus brothers an outright rejection, when their navigator Bartholomew Dias found a route to India around the tip of Africa in 1488. But, ever the optimists, the Columbuses turned that into an advantage by preparing a presentation to the kings of England and France pointing out that their route was shorter. Whether it was that idea or the prospect of foreign

Above: *The sea was full of terrors for Columbus and his men. But they sailed on for seventy days before sighting land.*

On October 12, 1492, they landed in the Bahamas on Guanahani, which Columbus renamed San Salvador.

competition that tipped the balance, Queen Isabella of Spain had Christopher stopped as he was about to board a ship to join his brother in Paris, and made an offer to finance an expedition across the Western Sea under her flag. She also offered him the title Admiral of the Ocean Sea, an honor he carried with him for the rest of his life.

His tenacious enthusiasm had gotten him that far, but it required the skills of a master mariner to go the rest of the way, and Christopher Columbus was one of the most skillful sailors who ever lived. Although he had championed the idea of sailing due west, it must have given the Queen's henchmen some anxious moments when his three ships cleared the port of Palos de la Frontera on August 3, 1492 and immediately turned south. He knew, but they didn't, that the prevailing northeasterly winds in the vicinity of the Canary Islands would blow his ships all the way to Japan, which was on the same latitude as the Canaries. He was right about the wind, but when they made a landfall on October 12, they were still a long, long way from Japan.

They were in the Bahamas, in fact, on an island

Right: *In the 16th century Elizabeth I of England challenged Spanish claims to the North American coast.*

the natives called Guanahani, but that Columbus renamed San Salvador.

In those days it was an article of faith that, at the Creation, God had made six-sevenths of the world dry land and that it was divided among three continents, Europe, Africa, and Asia, the latter being commonly known as "the Indies." No one, least of all Columbus, had any place in their philosophy for any other land mass. It was Marco Polo's descriptions of golden palaces and endless riches on the island of Cypangu, which is what he called Japan, that had prompted Isabella to finance the expedition, and the Admiral sincerely believed he had landed on an island close to his goal. His first move to offer proof was to call the natives "Indians," and his second was to begin collecting specimens of exotic plants that his ship's surgeon certified were native Asiatic flora. But there were slim pickings on San Salvador, and after two days of exploring the island, Columbus decided to keep on going in hopes of finding Japan, or possibly even China and the court of the Great Kahn himself.

With six of the Arawak natives as guides, the Spanish ships explored a half-dozen of the Bahamian islands because the Indians wore gold ornaments, and Columbus was as determined to discover where it came from as he was to find an Oriental face. There were plenty of other islands to visit and the Arawaks put an end to the aimless rambling when they suggested that the Spaniards may find the gold they were looking for in a place they called "Colba." In the meantime, the Europeans had made some subtle discoveries that would change the world more than they knew. They took samples of Indian corn and sweet potatoes, completely unknown in fifteenth-century Europe, and they were further intrigued by the hammocks the natives slept in. And when they reached Cuba, the natives there were smoking cigars.

There wasn't an Oriental potentate anywhere to be seen, but Columbus believed with all his soul that this Cuba was really a long peninsula at the southeastern corner of China, and he confidently told his men that it would be possible to walk from there back to Spain. They preferred to go by ship, but first there was yet another island to explore. Its ruler had sent Columbus a solid gold belt buckle along with an invitation to stop by, and it was a summons that couldn't be ignored. Convinced that the gift had come from the Emperor of Japan, the Admiral steered his ships into a cove on what is now the coast of Haiti. There were signs of gold, though not of any Japanese, but Columbus, who was so impressed by the place he named it Hispaniola – the Spanish island – found what he interpreted as a sign from God there. As they approached the shore, his flagship, *Santa Maria*, ran aground on a coral reef and sank. No hands were lost and most of her cargo was salvaged, and Columbus decided that it meant that God intended him to establish a settlement on the island. He had even provided the means in the form of the ship's timbers. A dozen crewmen volunteered to stay in the place they called Navidad because it had been established on Christmas Day, and then, on January 4, after recovering from the celebration welcoming the new year, 1493, the caravel *Nina*, commanded by Admiral Columbus, followed by the smaller *Pinta*, set sail for home. Their Caribbean cruise had lasted twelve weeks.

Within six months, long before word reached brother Bartholomew in Paris that their dream had come true, Columbus was on his way back to the Indies, this time with seventeen ships and more than twelve hundred men. They added the Lesser Antilles to the map, beginning with Dominica and winding through the Caribbean with stops in Marie-Galante, Guadalupe, St. Martin and St. Croix before reaching the Virgin Islands and Puerto Rico. They stopped again at Hispaniola, where Columbus discovered that the Indians had wiped out the little town he left behind. But the news didn't deter him from establishing another one, after which he sailed off to have another look at Cuba. Already convinced it was a peninsula, he didn't attempt to sail around it, but he explored all but about fifty miles of its coast before moving off in the direction of Jamaica, which his native guides had hinted might be a source of gold.

By the time he got back to Spain he had mapped most of the western Caribbean, but to the folks back home it was just more of the same. He had already shown them some plants they had never seen before, brought them some Indians to wonder at, and added parrots to the royal menagerie, but there was very little gold among his treasures, and without gold, what is a treasure after all? To make matters worse, scholars were beginning to hint that Columbus hadn't reached the Indies after all, and that there was a big land mass beyond those islands that probably wasn't Asia, either. But Columbus held fast to the view that if God had made more than three continents it would have ben revealed in the Scriptures, and after two years of hard selling, he managed to scrape together a fleet of six ships to go and prove what he believed.

After a brief stop at Trinidad, his party landed on the coast of South America near the delta of the

Left: *Sir Humphrey Gilbert was among the first Englishmen to plan an American colony. He lost his life in 1583 attempting to plant a settlement in Newfoundland.*

Orinoco River. The huge, freshwater bay was all the proof he needed that he had found a new continent, but that went against everything he believed, and he wrote that although he had always agreed with Ptolemy and others that the world was spherical, "… I have come to another conclusion … that it is not round as they describe but of the form of a pear." He went on to say that the globe seemed to have a protuberance south of the Equator that was no less a place than "the earthly paradise whither no one can go but by God's permission." It made perfect sense. The Book of Genesis said that the Garden of Eden was east of the point where the sun first appeared, and that it was the source of a river that parted into four heads. There before his eyes was the required four-headed river. The Bible also said that there was gold in the land watered by the first river, and the natives not only told him there was a vast land beyond, but that it was rich in gold. The force of the water rushing through the delta suggested it came from high mountains, which Columbus postulated must be the highest on earth, placing Eden at the spot closest to heaven, which rounded out his image of a pear-shaped planet. What he had found, he decided, was not a new world but, in his words, another world.

He made a fourth voyage in 1502 to find a connection with the Indian Ocean, but a search of the coast of Central America didn't produce one, and Columbus went to his grave never knowing that the Indian Ocean was still thousands of miles away across another sea he never dreamed existed. Nor did he ever know that he had discovered America. It was probably merciful that he never knew it would be named for a different man.

Left: *England's King James I signed the charter for his country's first successful American colony, the 1607 Jamestown settlement in Virginia.*

Facing page: *Jamestown was eventually joined by twelve other English colonies, all of which, along with Spanish Florida, became independent of foreign colonizers and proudly began calling themselves the United States of America.*

Right: *Although some dismiss Amerigo Vespucci as a fraud, there are solid reasons to honor him. He was the first to explore the South American coast, and first to describe it as a separate continent.*

Lettera di Amerigo vespucci delle isole nuouamente trouate in quattro suoi viaggi.

ANOTHER NAME FOR EDEN

Like the four-minute mile or a trip to the moon, once the impossible has been accomplished it begins to look easy. Within a few years of Columbus's first voyage a half-dozen others made the trip, including his brother, Bartholomew, who sailed to Hispaniola. Also among them was Alonzo de Ojeda, who had commanded one of the ships on Columbus's second voyage. Ojeda's goal was to collect pearls for a consortium of Sevillian merchants, but the master of one of his ships had something different on his mind. He was Amerigo Vespucci, a Florentine who, like Columbus, had made a lifetime study of the ancient map-makers and astronomers and was intrigued by the quest for a westward route to the East. Throughout American history, it has been fashionable to put Vespucci down as a fraud and a rascal who took all the credit for Columbus's accomplishments, but while Ojeda was off looking for pearls, Amerigo went off on his own to explore the coast of South America, reporting back that it was not only a separate continent but that, contrary to all previous scientific dogma, it was possible for humans to live in the Torrid Zone.

His contribution might have ended there, but on the other side of the world Pope Alexander VI, whose family, the Borgias, had come from Spain, issued a papal bull that gave all newly-discovered lands west and south of a line one hundred leagues from the Azores to Ferdinand and Isabella. The King of Portugal was incensed, and after a year of negotiations he managed to have the line moved another two-hundred-and-seventy leagues further west, but Spain still had the lion's share of the recently-discovered territory. In spite of it, South America seemed to have potential for the Portuguese, who had a claim of discovery after Pedro Alvares Cabral found the coast of Brazil, and King Manuel I turned to Vespucci to go and explore it. His voyage covered all but a few hundred miles of South America's entire Atlantic coast.

What made Vespucci different was that he was a flamboyant writer. Columbus had written extensively about his voyages, but as a gentleman in the service of a Catholic queen he had been especially conservative in his descriptions of the people he called Indians. He noted that the women had "very pretty bodies," that they wore nothing but gold jewelry, and that they "offered themselves freely," but generally steered clear of anything more graphic. Vespucci, on the other hand, went into greater detail, with the result that his writings made better reading.

But there was plenty in them to satisfy the scientifically-inclined, too, and among them was a clergyman named Martin Waldseemuller, who headed a scholarly society in Northern France. The group had a new printing press and was determined to produce an updated version of Ptolemy's geography, incorporating the new discoveries. But although Waldseemuller was an avid collector of geographical reports, he had none on Columbus's accomplishments. Government censorship kept all but the sketchiest information from crossing national boundaries, and the Spanish found it in their best interest to conceal any speculation that its explorers might have found a fourth continent. At the same time, Vespucci's reports had been published by his friend Lorenzo de Medici in Florence, and Waldseemuller had a copy. He was aware of rumors that Columbus and others had explored some offshore islands, but the atlas he was preparing was going to include the new continent, and it seemed to him that it was appropriate to name it for the person who described it so eloquently. And he had another reason that made the idea palatable to his fellow scholars. Both Europe and Asia were named for women, he pointed out, and it was high time that a man was represented on the map of the world. Their map was printed in 1507 with the new continent identified as "America." Within a few months they had printed and sold a thousand copies, but by

then new information prompted Waldseemuller to have second thoughts about Amerigo's real accomplishments and he removed the name in subsequent printings. It was too late. What the printing press had created other presses couldn't undo, and when Gerardus Mercator published his authoritative map of the world thirty years later, he not only reinstated Amerigo's name in South America but inscribed it on the land to the north as well. There was no turning back after that. Vespucci's book became the basic source of information on what he had identified as the New World, and for the rest of the sixteenth century the average European man in the street, even those who hadn't been titillated by Amerigo's graphic descriptions of life in the Torrid Zone, believed that he had discovered the lands that were named for him. But more important than who found them was the question of what was to be done with them. There was no shortage of ideas and almost all of them contained glimmerings of greed.

Above: *The French based their American claims on a 1524 voyage by the Italian Giovanni da Verrazano, who explored the coast north from the Carolinas.*

Facing page: *Verrazano's countrymen, John and Sebastian Cabot, had already claimed the northeast coast for England more than twenty-five years before he sailed past. Their 1498 voyage took them from Newfoundland to the Chesapeake Bay.*

Right: *In 1513, when Juan Ponce de Leon left to find the fountain of youth and discovered Florida instead, his home port on the island of Hispaniola already resembled an old and thriving Spanish city.*

MOVING IN

By the beginning of the sixteenth century it was obvious that Columbus and the others hadn't found the Indies after all, but a barrier that separated the riches of the East from Europe. Vasco Nunuz de Balboa had walked across Panama and discovered the Pacific Ocean in 1513, and six years later Ferdinand Magellan sailed around the tip of South America, proving once and for all that Asia was a long way from the so-called Indies. There was nothing for it but to make the best of what the Pope had decreed was theirs, and the Spanish rolled up their sleeves and went to work.

In the same year that Balboa hacked his way through the Panamanian jungle, one of Columbus's shipmates, Juan Ponce de Leon, who stayed on to become governor of the settlement on Hispaniola and later added Puerto Rico to his personal fiefdom, set out to find the island of Bimini, which the Indians told him contained a magical fountain that could wash away the ravages of age. He never found Bimini or the fabled fountain of youth but discovered Florida instead, and seven years later, on a second trip to determine whether it was a peninsula or an island, hostile Indians solved his problem of coping with old age by killing him. At almost exactly the same time, Hernando Cortes was leading an army of seven hundred men across the mainland into the land of the Aztecs, and establishing a Spanish presence in what would come to be known as Mexico. The natives were terrified, not only of his guns, but of the

Above: *When Ferdinand VII became Spain's king in 1808, his country's American empire started to crumble as revolutions spread from South America to Mexico.*

It didn't take very long for the natives to figure out what the newcomers wanted, and everywhere the Spanish went the Indian chiefs told them that they would find plenty of gold just over the next mountain or across the next river. The result was a century of exploration that mapped most of what was to become the southern part of the United States. It began in 1527, with a nine-year walk along the Gulf Coast from Florida and across Texas and Mexico to the Gulf of California, by Alvar Nunez Cabeza de Vaca. He claimed to have found gold and precious stones along the way, but rather than sending him back to get it, the Spanish king dispatched Hernando de Soto on a second expedition to secure his claim to sovereignty over the east coast of Florida which, as far as he was concerned, extended north as far as Newfoundland.

De Soto and his men marched north from Tampa Bay across Georgia and into South Carolina, where they became the first Europeans to see the Great Smoky Mountains. They turned south through Tennessee, following the Indians' directions to a great city on the site of present-day Tuscaloosa, Alabama, and eventually found the Mississippi River, which de Vaca also claimed to have discovered but de Soto was the first to describe. In his travels de Soto managed to alienate every Indian tribe he came in contact with, but although he didn't find any gold, he did find wild turkeys, and in return left behind hundreds of pigs, the descendants of a herd his men laboriously prodded along the entire line of march, making Southern barbecues inevitable.

Neither de Soto nor de Vaca wasted much effort bringing Christianity to the Indians, a goal high on the Spanish agenda, and they didn't show a lot of interest in describing the countryside or the plants and wildlife they found. Those scientific pursuits fell to the Jesuits, who joined a 1539 expedition led by a black man known as Estevan to explore the lands to the north. The priests were reassuring to the natives, but it was Estevan who impressed them most. A giant of a man with a full beard, he covered himself with bright feathers and bells and carried a feather-bedecked gourd as a symbol of power, a device he had picked up along with other secrets of the medicine men he had befriended in his explorations of Texas. He marched with a pair of greyhounds beside him, and was followed by a train of Indian women who carried his supplies and saw to his creature comforts. It goes without saying that he marched well ahead of the friars. The march took them into the plains of Kansas and Nebraska, where they saw great herds of bison, all carefully noted by

horses that carried his soldiers, the first of these animals that any of them had ever seen, and when the natives offered a king's ransom in gold and silver, the conquistadores enslaved them to dig up some more. A few years later, Francisco Pizarro marched down the west coast of South America and took an even bigger treasure from the Peruvian Incas. Less than a half-century later, the Spanish had established more than two hundred settlements in the Americas and 160,000 Spaniards were enjoying the fruits of the labors of more than a half-million Indian slaves.

Above: *After Isabella I of Castile married Ferdinand II of Aragon late in the 15th century, their united kingdom of Spain became a major world power.*

turned back toward Mexico. First, though, they noted in their journals that they had seen a great city off in the distance, surely one of the seven cities of Cibola that the Spanish had been told held greater treasure than those of the Aztecs and Incas put together. But looting cities wasn't part of their calling. That was a job for the governor himself, Don Francisco Vasquez de Coronado.

The expedition was an impressive one, with dozens of Spanish noblemen who had gone to Mexico looking for adventure, but when they reached the Zuni pueblo none of them was impressed. Instead of seven golden cities, they found seven adobe towns, and though they were surprised to find four- and five-story buildings there, Coronado noted that their own settlements in the south were far grander. But he wasn't a man who gave up easily. He believed the cities of gold must be out there somewhere and that it was his destiny to find them. The Indians, as usual, kept directing them to places just over the horizon, and in the process the Spaniards made some impressive discoveries, including the Grand Canyon and the Rocky Mountains. But what intrigued them most was that an Indian slave who had marched with them from Mexico came forward and told them he had been raised in a great city called Quivira, where ordinary people ate from dishes made of pure gold. Not only that, but this man they called El Turco generously offered to lead them there.

They should have become suspicious when El Turco told them not to overload their mules with supplies for the march across the plains. The animals would be needed, he said, to carry gold instead. But they took his advice, and as they roamed across the grasslands of West Texas the Indians backed up El Turco's story, saying that Quivera was not far off to the north. Coronado eventually found Quivera on the plains of Kansas, but the natives were as poor as any he had seen, and after strangling El Turco in payment for his deception he headed back toward Mexico. He was impressed by the lands he discovered and suggested to the Viceroy that it might be as productive as Spain itself. The Viceroy responded by stripping him of his titles. Coronado had added considerable territory to Spain's holdings, but as far as the Viceroy of New Spain was concerned it was a moot point, as the Pope had already given them title to the lands. He had no way of knowing that the King of England, for one, had become a Protestant with no fear of the excommunication threatened for violation of the Papal edict, or that, in spite of the threat, the King of France was already claiming the northern part of the continent as his own.

the Jesuits, and everywhere they went Estevan's gourd seemed to have magical power over the Indians. But when they reached the southwestern desert, Estevan's luck ran out. The Zunis who lived there regarded the gourd as a symbol of their enemy, the Apache. Estevan tried to talk his way out of the situation by explaining that he had been sent from Spain, but the chiefs knew that Spain was the land of the white man, and before he could convince them that he was a Moor and not an Apache, Estevan was dead.

But before he died he managed to get a warning back to the priests who were following, and they

Prom Lupi

Left: *French Huguenots, Protestants driven from their homeland, began settling Florida in 1560. The land was hospitable, but the Spanish Catholics were not, and the newcomers were driven from America, too.*

Above: *Sebastian Cabot sailed to the New World five years after Columbus's first voyage and claimed Newfoundland for his English employers.*

SOME OTHER COUNTRIES HEARD FROM

Five years after Columbus found the Bahamas, John Cabot sailed from Bristol and planted the English flag in Newfoundland. A year later he crossed the Atlantic again and followed the North American coast southward to the area of the Chesapeake Bay. He found a hostile countryside which he was certain wasn't Asia, and speculation began that the waterway Columbus was looking for in Central America was probably up there in the north. But the English King Henry VII had other things on his mind and, except for fishing fleets, no British ships followed in Cabot's wake.

Another quarter century passed before the French got around to joining the search for a Northwest Passage by sending Giovanni da Verrazano on a cruise that took him up the coast from the Carolinas to Newfoundland. Obviously a practical man, after failing to find the waterway he went south from there to Brazil, and established trading posts that gave the Portuguese a run for their money in the New World. He also planted a radical idea in the minds of Europeans when he suggested that the Americas ought to be colonized by the French. To be sure, the Spanish and Portuguese had already established colonies, but their concept was more like the ancient Romans, who conquered and occupied foreign territory but never considered themselves anything but citizens of Rome. The idea of calling America home never entered their minds.

But it wasn't an idea whose time had come. In 1534, another French explorer, Jacques Cartier, discovered the St. Lawrence River and, after wintering among the Indians near present-day Quebec, he decided it would be a good place to plant a colony, not because he liked the climate or the countryside, but as a base to attack the rich kingdoms the Indians assured him were just beyond the mountains. King Francis I was fascinated by the idea but, except for a few convicts and a force of soldiers, his subjects didn't seem interested. After one Canadian winter, even the convicts lost interest and Cartier's colony was abandoned.

Meanwhile, back in France, followers of John Calvin, who called themselves Huguenots, were converting thousands to Protestantism, and in an effort to get rid of the new heretics the French began making serious attempts at colonizing North America. None of their colonies took hold, mostly because they were in the southern latitudes, where the climate was not only better but where there were Spanish treasure ships to raid, an activity that invited retaliation. The Huguenot threat encouraged the Spanish to build more fortified towns, including St. Augustine in Florida, which stands today as the oldest European settlement in North America. The threat ended completely in 1572, when a bloody religious war in France drove the Huguenots underground, much to the relief of the Spanish in America, who had alienated the Indians so completely that their coastal outposts were in constant danger. And there was another danger just over the horizon. Many of the Huguenots found refuge in Protestant England, and their firsthand information about the Americas, along with their ideas of colonizing it, intrigued the British. The prospect of piracy against Spanish treasure ships added fuel to the fire and Queen Elizabeth's hatred of the Spanish made it the hope of England's future. Grand plans were made to establish a string of colonies between Florida and Newfoundland, and the Queen gave a charter to Sir Humphrey Gilbert to build the first of them. Along

Right: *Sixteenth-century Dutch explorers roamed the Caribbean and found some very good reasons to stay in the islands they discovered.*

with his half-brother, Walter Raleigh, and their cousin, Richard Grenville, he sponsored several voyages to find the right spot to begin, and Grenville put their first colony on Roanoke Island in the Outer Banks of the Carolinas in 1584. But, like others who had preceded them, the colonists gave up in less than a year and sailed for home. Raleigh decided that the Chesapeake was a better place to settle and sent colonists in that direction three years later, but the captain of their ship was interested in getting on to the Spanish Main for a bit of piracy and dropped his passengers at Roanoke instead. When they mysteriously vanished without a trace, the entrepreneurs gave up on the idea of populating America with Englishmen.

A war with Spain diverted Queen Elizabeth's attention, too, and when she wasn't looking the French established colonies along the northern coast, in territory the English claimed because their man Cabot had been there first. It was already a rich fishing ground for both countries, and the fur trade was beginning to make Europeans sit up and take notice. Once the war ended and piracy was made illegal, Englishmen became more interested in making an honest living in North America, and the idea of extending English influence beyond the sea became one of the Crown's top priorities. The seed was planted in 1606, when King James I granted a charter to a group of businessmen to settle the area his predecessor, Elizabeth I, had called Virginia in honor of herself, the Virgin Queen.

Their first colony at Jamestown got off to a shaky start, but it became relatively prosperous after the colonists found better ways to raise tobacco, the Indians' gift to Europe. It encouraged other English merchants to invest in the New World and to elbow the French and the Spanish aside, making the east coast of North America not only English-speaking, but Protestant as well.

Jamestown's savior during the early days, when disease and discouragement threatened to send the survivors home to England, was Captain John Smith, a tough-minded soldier of fortune who explored the surrounding territory, including the Potomac River. He also managed to make peace with the Indians, but he was forced to do it the hard way. He was taken prisoner by Powhatan, the Emperor of all the Chesapeake tribes, and spent his months of captivity entertaining the great chief's twelve-year-old daughter, Pocahontas. He had been an armorer in his military days and charmed the little girl, teaching her to make bells and jewelry while each learned the other's language. When her father finally decided to

Facing page: *When Sebastian Cabot explored the coast of Labrador, he didn't find much of value in the frozen North. But when Jacques Cartier (above) arrived at the Gulf of St. Lawrence in 1535, his fellow Frenchmen began to think that there could be riches for the taking in the interior.*

teenth century, settlers had been arriving at the rate of a thousand a year. Most found death rather than a new life, but it didn't stop others from following. There was also a small English colony in Newfoundland, and about fifteen-hundred Englishmen were prospering on plantations in Bermuda.

The fourth successful Anglo-American community was different from the others because the profit motive had nothing to do with it. The one-hundred-and-fifty people who landed at Provincetown on Cape Cod in 1620 were Separatists, a breakaway group of Protestants whose activities were outlawed in England. They had signed a contract with the Virginia Company, but by landing far north of its territory they were free to set up their colony to suit themselves. Less than ten years after they established their settlement at Plymouth, the Pilgrims managed to pay off their debt to the businessmen who financed their voyage, and had a clear title to all of Cape Cod and the islands of Nantucket and Martha's Vineyard, as well as the mainland north to Massachusetts Bay and west to Narragansett Bay. They made peace with the Indians and lived in a self-contained world where they made the rules and lived by them. Other Englishmen in general avoided their territory, but there were exceptions. Among them was an English aristocrat named Thomas Morton, who established a haven near Plymouth for indentured servants from other colonies who didn't want to fulfill their contracts. It was a noble undertaking in theory, but the freed slaves weren't at all interested in hard work, which was at the heart of Pilgrim belief. Instead they spent all their time drinking and carousing, and when Morton put a Maypole in the center of his town and word got back to the Pilgrims that naked Indian maidens were encouraged to dance around it, their governor, William Bradford, decided it was time something was done. A party of nine soldiers led by Captain Miles Standish marched on the town, which had the indecent-sounding name of Mare Mount, where they managed to capture Morton and, after tearing down the wicked Maypole, shipped him off to exile in England.

While all that was going on the colony's business agent was in London, and when he arrived back in Plymouth in 1629 he had a new secretary with him. The new recruit was a bit worldly by Pilgrim standards, but well-educated. He was well-known, too. It was Thomas Morton. Fortunately for him, there was a brand-new colony up on Massachusetts Bay and the Pilgrim fathers were pleased to send him there.

bring the white man to trial, his sentence was to have his brains dashed out. But before the first blow could be struck, Pocahontas put her own head on the execution stone and melted Powhatan's heart. He made the Captain his blood brother and peace existed between the English and the Indians from that moment until Powhatan died. Smith, in the meantime, moved on to greater things.

He was hired by another company of English merchants to explore the northern coast and, when he went back home, he wrote a book describing a wonderful place he called New England. It was an instant best-seller and his readers were inspired to go and live there. But by then the idea of emigrating to America had already taken hold. Although the population of Virginia was reduced to less than nine hundred by the second decade of the seven-

These pages: *After the Pilgrims arrived off Cape Cod in 1620, they first agreed to a set of rules which became the basis of American common law. It was called the Mayflower Compact for the ship that had brought them from England to begin a new life in the New World.*

TRANSPLANTING ENGLAND

The Pilgrims were the first immigrants to cross the Atlantic searching for more than a chance to get rich. Their goal became an important part of the American fabric, the right to be free from religious persecution, and with the exception of Morton, whose crime was having no religion at all, they were content to live and let live.

The seven hundred Puritans who arrived in 1630 and began building Boston were also looking for religious freedom, but they weren't willing to turn a blind eye to encroachment by people with any religion but their own. Their leader, John Winthrop, told his people that the trading company they had put together was to be the foundation of a spiritual "city upon a hill," and that "the eyes of all people are upon us." Like the Pilgrims, they were believers in the ideas of John Calvin, who preached that God decided the fate of every individual long before birth, and that anyone destined for hell couldn't avoid damnation. Others, on the other hand, were believed to be pre-selected for salvation.

Nearly all of the Protestants who emigrated to America, including the French Huguenots, the

Scottish Presbyterians and the Dutch Reformists, believed in Calvinist ideals, but none were as convinced they were God's Elect as the English Puritans. They weren't too sure about the others, but it seemed best to keep them on the outside looking in.

By the end of their first year, the settlements on Boston Bay had attracted more than two thousand Puritans, who arrived in family groups with tools and livestock and household goods. And at the center of each community was the church, whose pastor and elders had nearly as much authority as the magistrates, who were all devout churchmen themselves. Those who didn't conform with the established religion had a choice keeping their ideas

to themselves or risking expulsion. The situation was exactly the same for Puritans back home, except the shoe was on the other foot, and in the 1630s more than 75,000 people left England for America.

But they weren't all Puritans and not all of them headed for Massachusetts. As many as two-thirds of them migrated to the West Indies, with many more choosing Barbados than Winthrop's city upon a hill. John Winthrop was probably just as happy. Not all Puritans shared his vision. He established a strong central government separate from the church, but individual towns were more closely controlled by their church, and some of the ministers refused to march in step behind Winthrop or their fellow clerics. One of the earliest of the dissenters was Reverend

Above: *Turned out from Massachusetts after a disagreement with his fellow Puritan clergymen, dissident Roger Williams took his followers into the wilderness and created a new colony which he called Rhode Island.*

Thomas Hooker, who gathered his flock together and removed it to the Connecticut River Valley. In less than a year two other congregations followed them, and before long there were enough other dissenters in their midst to form their own government independent of Massachusetts Bay.

Hooker's followers in Hartford, and another large group in New Haven, were free of Boston's influence, but they were still Puritans, and if some of their ideas made Bostonians wince, they were at least considered decent neighbors. It wasn't quite the same with Roger Williams, the former pastor of the church at Salem who had used his pulpit to call for a separation of church and state. The idea horrified churchmen and statesmen alike, and Williams was banished into the wilderness, where he not only survived but started a new colony he called Providence Plantation, which ultimately become Rhode Island. He went on to shock the Puritans even more by establishing a Baptist church there and offering a warm welcome to other denominations, including the hated Catholics and the despised Quakers.

Among Williams's heresies was the idea that the English had no right to lands that belonged to the Indians. In general the natives hadn't been hostile, but their attitude changed as the white men began to march inland. In 1637 the Pequots took matters into their own hands, murdering white farmers in the Connecticut Valley, and in return the whites burned their village to the ground, killing four hundred of their people. After that, the Indians seemed chastened for almost forty years. Then all hell broke loose. Led by King Philip of the Wampanoags, the coastal tribes banded together to destroy outlying white settlements. Before long, no white settler from the coast of Maine to the Hudson River was safe from the Indians' wrath. Hundreds of whites were massacred and dozens of entire towns burned to the ground before Philip himself was killed and the tribes rounded up, to be sold as slaves in the West Indies.

It ended New England's Indian problem, but the people who were transplanting England into North America still faced the Mother Country's old enemies in the new land. Since 1603, when Samuel de Champlain began exploring the St. Lawrence River and encouraging settlement there and in the West, hundreds of Frenchmen had settled down in North America, and a century later the French controlled all the territory from the St. Lawrence and the Appalachians to the Great Plains and south to New Orleans. The Spanish were still in control of Florida

and the Gulf Coast, and the territory of the English colonies was cut in half by the Dutch in the Hudson River Valley.

The Dutch problem was eliminated in 1664, when Charles II gave their colony, without asking them first, to his brother the Duke of York. Fortunately for them, the Dutch colony of New Amsterdam was run by hard-nosed businessmen, who didn't find it cost-effective to invest in defense, and their city and its harbor fell to an English fleet without a shot being

Above: *Roger Williams bought the Rhode Island land from the Indians and declared that his colony was open to everyone. Even Catholics and Quakers were welcome in what was America's first example of religious freedom.*

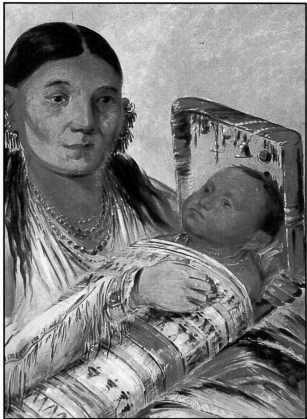

These pages: *William Penn's 1681 treaties with the Indians made Pennsylvania safe for generations, allowing* *colonists to roam into the interior unarmed and even to employ Indian women to take care of white children.*

fired. From that moment the English flag flew over all of the eastern seaboard from Maine to the Carolinas. But not all the new Americans came from England. The Dutch stayed on in New York as though nothing had happened, and when William Penn established his colony at Philadelphia after 1681, his haven for English Quakers, already the home of a large colony of Swedes, became America's first true melting pot.

Penn had a consuming dream but he wasn't an idle dreamer. After securing a huge land grant from the English king as payment of a family debt, he paid the Indians for the land he had been given and then offered it to prospective settlers. His fellow Englishmen were prime prospects, but the invitation to participate in what he called his Holy Experiment was extended throughout Scotland and Wales and into France, Switzerland and Germany. He was a master promoter, but the offer he made was too good to refuse no matter what the language. He

Above: *Most Native Americans were badly treated by the colonists, and cursed the day the whites arrived.*

Right: *Virginia Dare, the first English child born in America, was lost as a baby when the Roanoke Colony vanished.*

designed his city as a "green country town" with wide streets and large building lots, and he made it easy for farmers to acquire large tracts of productive land. He also made it simple for anyone to become a citizen of Pennsylvania, no matter where they came from or how they talked to God. And they came not only from all over Europe but from the other North American colonies as well. In less than twenty years, Pennsylvania was almost as large and possibly richer than either Virginia or Massachusetts, both of which had a head-start of well over fifty years.

Within another fifty years the French and the English were involved in a series of wars at home, and the American colonials were dragged into them. They were usually reluctant participants, but the fourth in the chain of world wars began in 1754, when a force of Virginia militia led by Colonel George Washington attacked French troops in the Ohio Valley. In Europe, it erupted into the Seven Years' War, pitting England and Prussia against France, Spain, Austria and Russia. In America, where the fighting had already been going on for two years, it was known as the French and Indian War. By the time it was over the French had been driven from North America, and although the lion's share of the fighting had been done by British troops, the colonials had given a good account of themselves, and if the English professionals found them rough around the edges, men from diverse colonies met and worked with one another and found they had a lot more in common than any of them had realized. They still represented thirteen distinct entities, but now that the French were removed from the other side of the Appalachians, they had a common goal. First, though, it would be necessary to remove the English from the eastern side.

Facing page: *A re-creation of a colonial washday in a time when the Puritan Fathers decreed that cleanliness was next to godliness.*

Left: *Hard work was an article of faith in the Massachusetts Bay Colony. But for the hardest jobs, it helped to have a yoke of oxen on hand.*

Above: *Virginia's Capitol at Williamsburg made some Englishmen wonder if they'd underestimated the people they regarded as "Colonials."*

Facing page: *If they complained about the price of imported maple sugar, the English didn't know how much work it took to produce or how cold it could get in the New England forest.*

Left: *No matter how much work there was to be done, the new Americans insisted that their children should take the time to learn to read and write.*

THE AMERICAN REVOLUTION

Everyone knows about the old woman who lived in a shoe, with so many children she didn't know what to do. The woman was Elizabeth Vergoose and she lived in colonial Boston. Her husband, Isaac, already had ten children when she married him and together they had ten more. When she became an old woman herself, she went to live with her daughter, who had fourteen children, and the little rhymes she made up for them earned her immortality as Mother Goose. There is no doubt she was an uncommon woman, but the size of her family was quite average for the times, and her little poem about the big family was a metaphor for the American condition. At the end of the French and Indian War, the population of the thirteen Eastern Seaboard colonies was about 1.6 million, and in a little more than twenty years the number doubled. They were all shoehorned into a relatively small area east of the Alleghenies, and

Above: *Before the English took over in 1664, the Dutch had spread far out of New Amsterdam into the surrounding countryside.*

Left: *In 1639, Connecticut River Valley settlers wrote The Fundamental Orders, the basic law of the Connecticut colony and America's first true constitution.*

although the territory to the west had been pacified, the British government declared it off-limits for settlement. The edict didn't sit well with colonists looking for better farmland, not to mention real estate speculators who felt deprived of a golden opportunity. Businessmen were also frustrated by laws preventing them from dealing with anyone but British merchants. The colonists felt they were being treated like stepchildren, but there was another insult on the way.

The English army had just won the Seven Years' War, expanding the British empire to undreamed-of proportions, but at the same time it also expanded Britain's national debt to unheard-of proportions. The fighting in America alone had added more than seventy million pounds to it, and London decided the time had come for the colonials to share some of the burden. They were maintaining a garrison of about 10,000 troops in North America and argued that, since they were protecting the colonists, the Americans should pay a third of the cost of keeping them there. The Americans disagreed, and when they dragged their feet in taxing themselves, Parliament forced one on them, requiring official stamps on printed items ranging from newspapers to playing cards to legal documents. The fees weren't

Below: The first British attempt to storm Fort Ticonderoga on Lake George failed, but they went on to win the French and Indian War.

ALL thofe who prefer the Glory of bearing Arms to any fervile mean Employ, and have Spirit to ftand forth in Defence of their King and Country, againft the treacherous Defigns of *France* and *Spain*, in the

Suffex Light Dragoons,

Commanded by

Lt. Col. John Baker Holroyd,

Let them repair to

Where they fhall be handfomely Cloathed, moft compleatly Accoutred, mounted on noble Hunters. and treated with Kindnefs and Generofity.

NEWS! NEWS!!

AARON OLIVER, *Poft-Rider*,

WISHES to inform the Public, that he has extended his Route ; and that he now rides thro' the towns of *Troy, Piltftown, Hoofick, Mapletown*, part of *Bennington* and *Shaftfbury, Petersburgh, Stephentown, Greenbufh* and *Schodack*.

All commands in his line will be received with thanks, and executed with punctuality.

He returns his fincere thanks to his former cuftomers ; and intends, by unabated diligence, to merit a continuance of their favours.

O'er ruggid hills, aud vallies wide,
He never yet bas fail'd to trudge it :
As fteady as the flowing tide,
He bands about the NORTHERN BUDGET.

June 18, 1799.

Above: *Among the men who served the British Army against the French in 1754 was Colonel George Washington of the Virginia Militia.*

Far left: *Handbills urged Englishmen to defend their King and Country in the Seven Years' War, which in America was called the French and Indian War.*

Left: *After the war, the English controlled all of Canada and today's United States east of the Mississippi, giving plenty of new work for post-riders.*

Above: *English taxes they thought onerous, beginning with the Stamp Act of 1765, brought American Colonials together for angry protests.*

large, but they affected nearly everyone, and many felt that if they paid this tax others would surely follow.

It started the colonies in the direction of uniting for the first time when leaders from nine of them met together to draft a formal protest to London. It also united the people who took to the streets with anti-tax demonstrations and started a spontaneous boycott of British imports. The demonstrations made life unpleasant for tax collectors and other officials, and the boycotts had a serious effect on the English economy. The result was repeal of the Stamp Act, which gave the colonists confidence in the idea that if they were united they had power. But the power

they were up against was formidable and it wasn't taking their protest lying down.

Parliament replaced the stamp tax with a tariff on glass, lead, paper and tea which, because it was paid by importers, didn't affect the man in the street except through higher prices. But it brought the people into the streets again, and when the British sent troops to Boston to put them in their place, a minor riot produced eleven civilian casualties. It was the first blood that was drawn in the growing family feud between England and her American colonies, and it galvanized the rebels into establishing secret committees to coordinate protests among the different colonies. They came

out in the open near the end of 1773, when bands disguised as Indians descended on harbors from Virginia to Massachusetts and destroyed thousands of chests of tea waiting to be unloaded from British ships. Parliament singled out Boston for punishment by closing its port, and at the same time it solved a problem in Canada by extending Quebec's boundary southward into the Ohio Valley and giving the French among them the right to take their Catholic religion into the new territory. New Englanders were appalled. Not only was Massachusetts out of business, but territory they considered theirs had been taken from them and given to the hated Catholics. As far as they were

concerned, if Satan had a human form it was as England's King George III.

Their neighbors agreed, and delegates from all the colonies except Georgia met in Philadelphia to decide what should be done. Parliament turned a deaf ear to their list of grievances and up and down the coast bands of local militia began drilling on village greens and in town squares. Then, in April, 1775, British soldiers sent from Boston to capture the rebels John Hancock and Samuel Adams met a band of colonial Minutemen at Concord Bridge, and soon the family feud turned into full-scale war.

If the war had been covered on television, the experts on the evening news would have been

Above: *Protesting a British monopoly on tea, Bostonians disguised as Indians dumped 342 chests of the "cursed weed" into the harbor in 1773, in an event that became famous as the "Boston Tea Party."*

Above: *In Virginia, Thomas Jefferson, Patrick Henry and others put their protests against "English tyranny" in writing.*

Facing page: *In Boston, rebels faced British guns and were "massacred" in a 1770 skirmish that left eleven citizens killed or wounded.*

and most of them went home after a few months. When the war finally ended, the Continental Army was only about seventy-five-hundred strong. When it started, the individual colonies still weren't truly united and regional differences made it impossible for them to agree on a concerted course of action. And in the early stages of the fighting the British occupied Boston, New York and Philadelphia, which in a traditional war would have been regarded as a signal of early victory. But this was not a traditional war.

After the skirmish at Concord all thirteen colonies sent delegates to the Second Continental Congress in hopes that they could head off a full-scale war. But just to be on the safe side, they authorized the creation of an army and a navy and appointed George Washington to take charge of the defense of Boston. By the time he arrived there, the Massachusetts Minutemen had scored a stunning victory in the bloody battle of Bunker Hill, and England had formally declared war on her American colonies. Still, the majority of Americans felt that war was the height of foolishness and a full year went by before Congress decided to take Benjamin Franklin's advice that if they didn't hang together they would surely hang separately. And with Thomas Jefferson's dramatic Declaration of Independence, the die was cast on July 4, 1776.

The war went badly for the rebels until October, 1777, when the British General John Burgoyne surrendered his army to the Americans led by Horatio Gates at Saratoga, New York. The victory isolated British troops in Canada and prompted Parliament to raise a white flag in the form of an offer of home rule, but not independence, for the colonies. The offer was rejected, but it raised eyebrows in Paris, where the French leaders saw an opportunity to break up the British Empire. They had been providing covert help all along, but early in 1778 they came out into the open by signing a treaty with the Americans, pledging their help against the common enemy. It wasn't long before England and France were at war again in Europe, and before much longer both Spain and Holland were attacking British ships. The American Revolution, like the French and Indian War, had become a world-wide conflict.

The addition of French regulars, along with the harassment of British supply ships, boosted American morale, but the war was far from over. It finally came to an end in 1781, when the French fleet blockaded Chesapeake Bay and Washington's army, augmented by French troops, cornered the British at Yorktown, Virginia, and forced them to surrender. In the treaty

predicting that nothing could possibly come of it. England was the most powerful country on earth, with a legendary navy and an army of 50,000 seasoned professionals, and it had the money to hire as many mercenaries as might be needed. In spite of the number of different reasons for colonials of various stripes to support a break with England, thousands were loyal enough to the Mother Country to join the other side, and along with them the English recruited several thousand Indians to keep up pressure on the frontier. The colonial soldiers, on the other hand, were poorly trained and badly supplied, and out of several hundred thousand able-bodied men only seventy or eighty thousand actually volunteered,

The BLOODY MASSACRE perpetrated in King—L Street BOSTON on March 5th 1770 by a party of the 29th REGT.

Engrav'd Printed & Sold by PAUL REVERE BOSTON

Unhappy BOSTON! see thy Sons deplore,
Thy hallow'd Walks besmear'd with guiltless Gore:
While faithless P—n and his favage Bands,
With murd'rous Rancour stretch their bloody Hands;
Like fierce Barbarians grinning o'er their Prey,
Approve the Carnage and enjoy the Day.

If scalding drops from Rage from Anguish Wrung
If speechless Sorrows lab'ring for a Tongue,
Or if a weeping World can ought appeafe
The plaintive Ghosts of Victims such as these:
The Patriot's copious Tears for each are shed.
A glorious Tribute which embalms the Dead

But know FATE summons to that awful Goal.
Where JUSTICE strips the Murd'rer of his Soul:
Should venal C—ts the scandal of the Land,
Snatch the relentless Villain from her Hand,
Keen Execrations on this Plate inscrib'd,
Shall reach a JUDGE who never can be brib'd.

The unhappy Sufferers were Messrs. SAML. GRAY SAML. MAVERICK, JAMS. CALDWELL, CRISPUS ATTUCKS & PATK. CARR
Killed. Six wounded; two of them (CHRIST. MONK. & JOHN CLARK) Mortally

that was signed two years later, England recognized her former colonies as an independent nation and established its boundaries to the Mississippi River in the west and from the Great Lakes south to Florida.

The United States of America. It had a nice ring to it, but the states were still a long way from being united when the shooting stopped. Under their Articles of Confederation, Congress had no authority except the right to its own opinion that the states could disagree with, and they often did. And even more often they disagreed among themselves. Nearly all the states taxed goods produced in other states as though they were foreign countries. Connecticut claimed land in Northeastern Pennsylvania, and though Congress ruled in favor of the Pennsylvanians, the New Englanders got out their guns. Pennsylvania, meanwhile, was also at odds with Virginia over its claim to territory stretching due west from Philadelphia into Indiana, and land speculators from several states were challenging the Carolinians' right to sovereignty over their western frontier.

When the British left, nearly one hundred thousand Loyalists left with them. By and large, colonists who supported the Mother Country were the ones with the most to lose in a revolution, including successful merchants and businessmen, educated professionals and large landowners. In losing them, American lost not only capital and valuable experience, but a cultured upper level of society that might have become a source of needed leadership and a conservative counterbalance to the radical ideas of the former rebels.

Loyalist property, as well as former Crown lands, was confiscated and sold by speculators who became America's new rich and behaved accordingly. They did all they could to impress their neighbors with displays of wealth, and were more effective in winning minds than the combined efforts of the Sons of Liberty and the Committees of Correspondence a decade earlier. One of those early revolutionaries noted the trend in a report that many contemporary Americans might find relevant today: "The system of politics remains much as it has been," he wrote, "the same imbecility, the same servility and the same inattention still prevail .... Money is the only object attended to, and the only acquisition that commands respect." In many cases, more than the pursuit of luxury was involved. Merchants, in their eagerness to get rich, were adding unconscionable profit margins to their prices, adding to the grief of a middle class already caught in an inflationary squeeze.

Among the hardest-hit were small farmers, many

Above: *New York, captured by the British in the 1776 Battle of Long Island, was occupied for the rest of the war.*

Facing page: *After the war, Shays' Rebellion in Massachusetts pitted farmers against bankers and tax collectors.*

Right: *"First in war, first in peace." Charles W. Peale captured both qualities of the general who became president in his portrait of George Washington.*

Above: *Tar and feathers were often all a tax agent collected in the days when revolution was in the air.*

Top right: *Francis Scott Key gave America something to sing about with his inspiring words for the* Star Spangled Banner.

of whom had served in the war and been paid with next to worthless money or not at all. They came home to mountains of debt they couldn't pay and found their income reduced in the bargain. In 1786, a group of them in Northwestern Massachusetts shocked the Establishment by picking up their guns and marching on courts they perceived to be favoring their creditors. The State responded by calling out the militia, and the little war known as Shays' Rebellion ended after a few skirmishes that left several farmers dead. But the upper classes got the message. It was a sign that the country was on a high road to anarchy, and they decided the time had come to establish a strong central government. The poorer classes, sensing that federalism was another word for authority, and that it would make foreclosures easier than ever, argued in favor of strengthening

state governments. But they all agreed that something needed to be done.

Congress responded by calling for a convention to revise the Articles of Confederation, but by the time the delegates arrived at Philadelphia they had already decided among themselves to forget about a confederation of sovereign states and to strengthen the federal government. It was easier said than done, but after seventeen long weeks of debate and compromise they produced a constitution that still needed to be approved by the states, whose power it proposed to curb. The people, as it turned out, weren't at all impressed.

The men who wrote the document: James Madison and George Washington, Alexander Hamilton and Benjamin Franklin, among others, were among the elite of the new country. Most of them were lawyers, some were merchants and all were comparatively wealthy. The firebrands of the Revolution weren't represented, nor were the poor farmers or the middle class. Fortunately for America, none of the fifty-five men who worked through the summer of 1787 to form the new Government put personal interest above the common good, but when Congress submitted the new Constitution to the states without comment, a majority of the people agreed with Virginia's Patrick Henry, who had boycotted the Constitutional Convention in the first place because he said he "smelled a rat."

The document was approved by nine states, the required two-thirds majority, the following spring, but it took arm-twisting, back room deals and agile politicking on the part of the Federalists to make it happen. Even with approval, they didn't have a solid majority on their side and there were still four states outside the pale. Virginia fell into line by ten votes, and New York by three within a few weeks, but North Carolina and Rhode Island held out until long after the new government was in place.

What finally bound them together was the electoral college's unanimous vote for George Washington as the country's first president. The framers of the Constitution had considered it a foregone conclusion, but with one notable exception, for General Washington didn't want the job. At fifty-six, he felt that he was too old. He was worried about his health and the deteriorated state of his Virginia plantation, and he was concerned that he would become a lightning rod for Anti-Federalist propaganda that would ruin his reputation.

These pages: *From frontier hero in 1758 to the man of the hour in '76, George Washington was the right man at the right time.*

But even George Washington could be wrong. With the exception of Benjamin Franklin, who was indeed too old, he was the only American with a truly national constituency, and after months of gentle persuasion by Alexander Hamilton and others, the General agreed to come out of retirement and went to New York, where, on April 30, 1789, he nervously swore to uphold the Constitution of the United States.

But the Constitution was silent on how he should

Below: John Adams wasn't one of the 55 members of the Constitutional Convention when it met in 1787, but his ideas guided those who were.

go about it. Washington's first job was to invent the presidency, and he began by creating a three-man cabinet which, along with Vice President John Adams, was to be his board of advisors. The men he chose were all his close friends, but there wasn't a yes-man among them, and Alexander Hamilton, the Treasury Secretary, and Secretary of State Thomas Jefferson had totally different ideas about both finance and foreign policy. Those differences corrected another Constitutional deficiency: Hamilton's followers became known as Federalists and Jefferson's as Democratic-Republicans, and the citizens of the United States were divided into political parties for the first time.

The Constitution had also been silent on individual rights, an oversight that became the first order of business for the new Congress. They drafted a dozen amendments, ten of which were quickly ratified by the states as a Bill of Rights. But the anti-federalists sneered, saying they'd had all those rights all along and they were still opposed to the big, bad central government. And they might have succeeded in

Facing page, top: James Madison, a leading force behind the Constitution, worked with Alexander Hamilton in writing The Federalist Papers *to help secure its ratification.*

Below: *Another future president, Thomas Jefferson, wrote the Declaration of Independence, proclaimed at Philadelphia on July 4, 1776.*

toppling it if President Washington hadn't been willing to use force against them. After Congress imposed a luxury tax on whiskey, people in Western Pennsylvania, who didn't consider the stuff a luxury at all, began giving tax collectors coats of tar and feathers instead of the revenue they came for. In defense of the rebels, it should be pointed out that whiskey was a medium of exchange in those parts, but on the other hand, it isn't likely that any of the locals invited a tax man in for a drink. Real trouble began when farmers shouldered their rifles and marched toward a house owned by a federal marshal. He had been warned in advance and was waiting for them with a band of armed men, who killed one of the farmers and wounded five. The next day they came back and burned the house down, and what became known as the Whiskey Rebellion was in full swing. Before it was over, the President called up the militias of several States, and to everyone's surprise 13,000 men responded, even though the common wisdom was that no state soldiers would ever cross the sacred lines into other states. Washington himself led them part of the way, and by the time they arrived the moonshiners had decided it was better to pay the tax than to face such an army. It gave them all, and others who would follow in their footsteps, a new respect for the federal government, and it gave all America the idea that what they had created was a people's government, and that the people could change it with their votes. It was one of the rights the Constitution gave them.

The Constitution also gave the president the right to negotiate treaties with the advice and consent of the Senate and it gave Congress the power to declare war, but it wasn't specific on the subject of conducting foreign policy. The Founding Fathers had hoped the subject wouldn't come up for several generations, but on July 14, 1789, exactly ninety-six days after Washington became president, the citizens of Paris stormed the Bastille, announcing a revolution that affected much more than the future of France. It forced the Americans to look beyond their borders, and the job of steering the course fell to the president himself. Few presidents have ever faced a tougher challenge.

Many of the men who had helped America during its own revolution, including the Marquis de Lafayette, eventually became victims of the upheaval, and many Americans were appalled at the Reign of Terror that followed it. On the other hand, Americans had demonstrated to the world that they were opposed to the rule of monarchs, and they didn't care to be put in the position of siding against other

such revolutionaries. Washington held firm on a policy of non-involvement, but a movement to restore the monarchy made that impossible. The French Republicans, citing the treaty that brought their help during the American Revolution, demanded help in return. American ships, meanwhile, were being threatened by the British, who were at war with France again; and Spain, which had also declared war on France, was in danger of losing her possessions in Louisiana. Washington tried to cool the situation in his own country by declaring a policy of strict neutrality, but it was easier said than done. Both France and England went right on highjacking American ships, and pressed the sailors into their own navies. The president responded by expanding his own navy, but it was hardly conduct becoming to a neutral power and it became obvious that diplomacy was in order.

When Washington sent John Jay to England to negotiate a treaty, it became the greatest test of his popularity. His people may not have been completely enamored of the French, but the late war had made most of them suspicious of the English, too, and most people felt that Jay's treaty was much too pro-British for anything good to come of it. But Washington signed it anyway and his reputation survived. So did the country. The people hated what Jay had done, but it kept them out of a war they couldn't afford, a prospect they wouldn't have to face for another seventeen years, during which time the territory of the United States would more than double, and its population would grow from less than four million to well over seven million.

These pages: Seamstress Betsy Ross is said to have created the Stars and Stripes, but there is no official record. Congress authorized the flag in 1777 to replace a banner that had a British Union Jack in the upper left corner and the new version joined the Continental Army.

Left: *The first major battle of the Revolution began when the Colonials, outnumbered two to one, took Boston's Bunker Hill from the Redcoats.*

Above: *The citizens of Boston watched the fighting across the bay from their rooftops. When the battle ended, King George III declared war on his colonies.*

Overleaf: *After the Continentals had retreated to Valley Forge, General Washington endured the Pennsylvania winter with his troops.*

GEORGE WASHINGTON AT YORKTOWN

The fall of Yorktown—October 19, 1781—was the deciding victory in America's war for independence. The painting shows General Washington looking toward Yorktown; behind him is Rochambeau, whose co-operation made victory possible. The ships of de Grasse lie in York River, and an English vessel is burning.

Facing page: *The war dragged on for five years before Washington and his French allies cornered the British at Yorktown, Virginia, and forced their surrender.*

Right: *Fighting raged in all the Colonies during those years. Meanwhile, Spain and Holland had declared war abroad, threatening the British in their own homeland.*

Left: *It all began with "the shot heard 'round the world" on April 18, 1775, when Redcoats fired on Minutemen at Concord, Massachusetts.*

Overleaf: *A major turning point was the British defeat at Princeton, New Jersey, after Washington surprised them in their winter camp.*

Above: *Architect, inventor, scientist, writer and statesman, Thomas Jefferson was America's first true renaissance man.*

Right: *Jefferson made the purchase that raised the American flag over the Louisiana Territory, more than doubling the size of the United States.*

Facing page: *James Monroe and Robert Livingston made the $15 million purchase of Louisiana official in 1803.*

COMING OF AGE

Americans have come to believe that their lives are regulated by the calendar. In our century, the twenties roared and the thirties whimpered; the sixties belonged to the radicals and the eighties to the self-serving. But one of the most dramatic examples of the calendar's effect on American life was the turn of the 19th century.

Thomas Jefferson was elected to the presidency in 1800, but tied with Aaron Burr in the electoral vote and became the first chief executive chosen by the House of Representatives, made up, ironically, of old aristocratic Federalists and not the common men Jefferson appealed to most. It was the death knell of their party and the start of a new era.

Within a few months of Jefferson's inauguration, which was the first held in the new federal city in the District of Columbia, Spain signed a secret treaty with France ceding New Orleans and the territory west of the Mississippi to Napoleon Bonaparte of France. The Spaniards had already closed the port to Americans, but their hold was weak, and Jefferson was sure they could be dislodged when the appropriate time came. But Napoleon was quite a different matter. Thomas Jefferson was a pacifist to the depths of his soul and, although he had authorized America's first foreign war against the Barbary Pirates in Tripoli and scored a dramatic victory, he didn't have the stomach to tangle with the legendary First Consul of France.

But he had an idea. After convincing Congress to allocate two million dollars, he sent James Monroe to join forces with Ambassador Robert Livingston in Paris to buy the city of New Orleans. Napoleon wasn't interested in selling anything, but not long after Madison arrived a slave revolt in Haiti made the island of Santo Domingo useless as a staging area for Napoleon's planned settlement of Louisiana, and a buffer against British attacks on his colony, and he abruptly changed his mind. There was a catch, though. If the Americans wanted New Orleans, said Napoleon, they'd have to take the whole territory and the price, including still-outstanding war debts, was twenty million dollars. Monroe and Livingston managed to negotiate the figure down to fifteen million, still a far cry from the original appropriation, but instead of just a city they were buying 828,000 square miles of territory as well, an area much larger than France itself.

The Federalists were violently opposed to the Purchase, largely because they saw that new states carved out of the Louisiana Territory would become Slave States, and by upsetting the balance they would make the South the dominant political force in the United States. But the people themselves, land-hungry from the beginning, were all in favor of it, and the Federalist Party was swallowed up in their enthusiasm. The euphoria was enhanced in 1804,

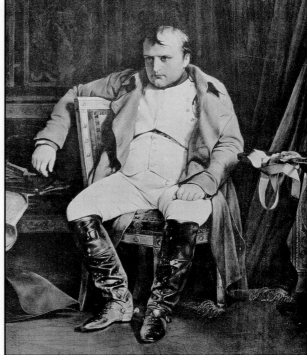

Left: *The Louisiana Purchase was welcomed on the frontier, as 828,000 square miles became United States territory.*

Above: *Napoleon Bonaparte, who sold what he considered to be useless wilderness to the Americans.*

when an expedition led by Jefferson's personal secretary, Meriwether Lewis, and his friend William Clark, set out to explore the Missouri River and find a water route across the continent.

The forty-five men who made the trip were all veterans of frontier army posts, but one of them was a French-Canadian trapper, Toussaint Charbonneau, whose Indian wife, Sacagawea, and their six-month old son went along with him. Sacagawea, the Bird Woman, was the sister of the chief of the Shoshonis. She had been kidnapped by the Mandans and sold to Chabonneau as a slave. Even though he had two other wives he married the girl, which was a break for Lewis and Clark because their route took them through Shoshoni country which she knew well and where she was well-known. And because she had a papoose strapped to her back, other tribes were reassured that this was no war party. Probably her most important contribution was in the way she faced the rough weather and tough country. It was a life-saving inspiration to the men, who would sooner die than give up in the face of conditions that didn't seem to faze a young woman.

Above: *In 1804, the Lewis and Clark Expedition pushed up the Missouri River and crossed the plains and the Rocky Mountains on their way to the Pacific Coast to explore the territory Jefferson had bought from France. This drawing is by Patrick Cass, one of the members of the Expedition.*

Most of the Indians they encountered had never seen a white man before, none had ever seen a black man. Captain Clark provided that experience in the person of his personal slave, a giant of a man named York, who was later described as "the observed of all observers, the curiosity of all the party." Both Lewis and Clark reported in their journals that they were frequently able to distract suspicious Indians with the promise of showing them a black man. The Indians, of course, didn't believe what they saw and routinely tried to rub the paint from York's body. As proof he was no hoax, they were encouraged to study his scalp through his hair, a rather dangerous suggestion considering the Indians' penchant for collecting scalps as souvenirs. But his size alone discouraged any such ideas they may have had, and he added to their trepidation by telling them he was originally a wild animal tamed by Captain Clark. To back it up, he'd make angry faces and roar, a demonstration which Clark wrote "made him more terrible than we wished." He also attracted unusual attention from the Indian women. A Cayuse woman in Oregon who had been fifteen when the party

reached there was interviewed on her hundred-and-tenth birthday and couldn't remember a thing about the arrival of the Lewis and Clark Expedition except that "there was a black man."

Jefferson had instructed the explorers to treat the Indians with dignity, a policy that would change in later years, and every encounter began with an invitation for a council of peace. The first of them, at Council Bluffs, Iowa, set the pattern for most of the others. Six chiefs of the Oto and Missouri tribes met with the whites in a tent made from the sail of one of their keelboats. Once the speechmaking was over, a peace pipe was passed among them, and the Americans distributed gifts of flags and medals, bits of clothing and colorful certificates inscribed with the name of the Great White Father, Mr. Jefferson, and the individual chief who received it. Like the Wizard of Oz, the American Captain explained that what separated leaders from ordinary men was often nothing more than a piece of paper. The chiefs couldn't read what was written on it, of course, but they were reassured that it identified them as true leaders of men. Once the ceremonies were over, the

Drawn with the Camera Lucida by Capt.ⁿ B.Hall R.N.

Engraved by W H.Lizars

chiefs were dazzled with demonstrations of such wonders as a magnet and a spyglass and, with the exception of York, the greatest wonder of all, an air rifle. Then, as a final clincher, a bottle of whiskey was passed around and then, with a request to pass the word among other chiefs that the white men were friendly, the expedition was on its way.

The powwows were all friendly until the boats entered the territory of the Sioux in South Dakota. When the Americans handed out their gifts, the chief, who appeared to be drunk, punched Clark and, after complaining that he had given them cheap junk, announced that the Expedition had reached the end of the line. The riverbank was lined with Sioux braves, but Clark drew his sword, Lewis unveiled a cannon and the men took aim with their long rifles. With that, the chief suddenly sobered up and ordered his men to put down their bows. The following day the whites were honored with a tribal feast, but it turned out to be a trick. The chief planned to kill them all as a climax to the celebration. When he asked for a ride in one of their boats, he turned hostile again, but Clark was ready for him. After

unceremoniously putting the chief ashore, he turned his cannon in the direction of the Indian village and gave the order for the boats to head upstream fast. The Indians followed them, but soon gave up the chase and the ordeal was over. Meanwhile, word went out to other tribes that these Americans couldn't be bullied, and the explorers had no more Indian problems as they followed the river across the Plains.

On the way, they collected specimens of plant and animal life and they swatted mosquitoes. They collected all kinds of Indian artifacts from pottery to buffalo robes, and they swatted more mosquitoes. By the time they got to the Continental Divide, they had already become the first white men to tangle with grizzly bears, and they found a new menace in the form of thousands of rattlesnakes, which made them forget all about the mosquitoes. When they reached the Rockies the river tumbled down in a waterfall so powerful they could hear its roar ten miles away. They obviously needed to go around it, but for that they needed horses. They had been told that the natives in the area had plenty to sell, but the Indians were nowhere to be found. From early April,

Above: *The original intent of the Louisiana Purchase was to buy New Orleans and give the United States access to the Mississippi River. But Napoleon forced the Americans to buy the whole territory in order to gain possession of the city.*

Above: *Most of the men who drafted the Constitution were under forty, but among them was eighty-one-year-old Benjamin Franklin.*

Right: *The building of the Erie Canal in 1825 connected New York with the Great Lakes, opening up the territory beyond.*

when they left their winter camp, until mid-June when they reached the mountains, they hadn't seen a single red man, hostile or otherwise. It took them a month to drag their gear around the falls, and then they had to face the prospect of crossing the mountains without horses.

They probably wouldn't have made it if they hadn't stumbled across an old Indian woman and two young girls, who led them to their village for a conference with their chief. But he was much more interested in their guide than in the white men. Sacagawea was his sister. She had been carried off five years earlier as an eleven-year-old girl and now she was a young woman. And she had come home. The negotiations that produced thirty horses were laborious because of the language problem. Sacagawea spoke Shoshone, but not English. Her

husband didn't speak English, either, and all the conversations were translated first into the language of the Plains Indians, which Charbonneau understood, and then into French for another member of the party, who translated it again for the Americans.

By then they were beyond the boundary of the Louisiana Purchase, but it had always been their goal to explore the Oregon Territory, where the Americans had established a shaky claim. It was the first week in November before they spotted the Pacific Ocean, and they established a winter camp near the mouth of the Columbia River. The following March they were ready to retrace their steps and, in September 1806, two years, four months and nine days after they left, the Lewis and Clark Expedition, minus one man who had died of appendicitis, was back in St. Louis.

In 1805, as Lewis and Clark were exploring the Yellowstone River on their way back to civilization, the British Admiral Lord Nelson smashed the combined French and Spanish fleets at Trafalgar off the coast of Spain, and Britannia ruled the waves from then on. But their enemy, Napoleon, who had indirectly made the Lewis and Clark Expedition possible, was still in control of the European land mass. The English decreed that no merchant ship could enter a French-controlled port without first stopping at a British port, and Napoleon counter-decreed that all ships entering British ports would be seized. The prime victims of both edicts were ships flying the American flag. It appealed to the American sense of adventure, and although a considerable number of ships were lost, it was considered one of the costs of doing business. But the British had always had a nasty habit of kidnapping sailors and pressing them into their own service, and by the end of the decade animosity toward the English, which had never been far beneath the surface, was erupting in calls for another war against the Mother Country.

Above: *The Dominion of Canada was formed with the union of British Upper Canada and French Lower Canada in 1849. It was a British colony until 1931, becoming independent with the Constitution of 1982.*

Right: *The continental borders of the United States were finalized by 1853, when the Gadsden Purchase added a strip of the Southwest that the Americans wanted as a right-of-way for a transcontinental railroad.*

Below: *England claimed all of Canada with the taking of Quebec in 1759.*

Overleaf: *Before the U.S.S.* Constitution *sank the British frigate* Guerriere *during the War of 1812, the English Navy had fought 200 battles without losing a single ship.*

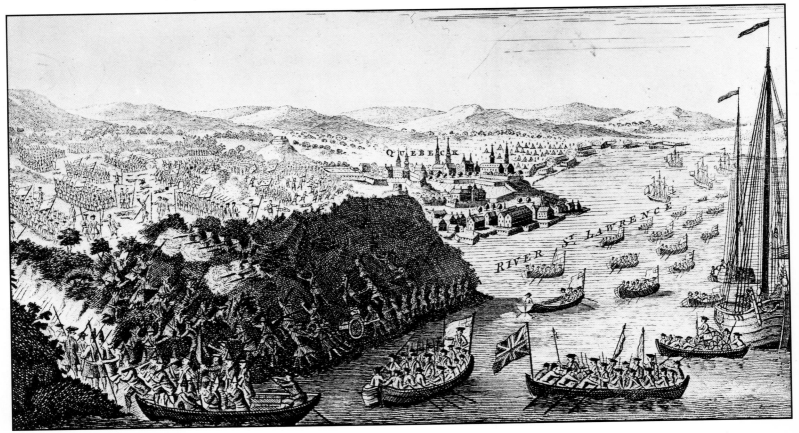

Left: *The British burned the city of Washington, D.C., on August 24, 1814, seriously damaging all its public buildings, including the White House.*

Right: *The Americans tried to invade Canada three times during the War of 1812, but were driven off, more often by the Canadians than by the British.*

When it finally broke out, the country was not only miserably unprepared for a war, but the people were hopelessly divided. Flags flew at half-mast in New England, where farmers drove their cattle into Canada to feed the British army. The annexation of Canada itself was one of the American goals, and their generals, who hadn't even thought about military strategy for thirty years, proposed a three-pronged invasion. The first attacking force moved out from Detroit, but quickly retreated and then surrendered without firing a shot. The New York militia was scheduled to cross the Niagara River but refused to leave their home state when they heard enemy guns on the other side; and the third army, which headed for Montreal along Lake Champlain, turned back when word reached them that they'd be on their own once they crossed the border. The following year they were repelled again, but an American fleet commanded by Oliver Hazard Perry managed to take control of Lake Erie, cutting the British off from the west. But the Americans were still on the defensive and, with the defeat of Napoleon in 1814, thousands of seasoned British troops were sent to North America to teach the Colonials a lesson. An American fleet on Lake Champlain managed to cut off their approach from the north, but another force put ashore from the Chesapeake Bay marched on Washington, where they set fire to most of the public buildings, including the White House, sending President James Madison into the surrounding hills.

Their next target was Fort McHenry at Baltimore, where they were beaten back, much to the delight of Francis Scott Key, who watched the battle from the deck of a British ship and was pleased to see, as he put it, "by the dawn's early light … that our flag was still there." But if the Star-Spangled Banner was still gallantly waving, the war wasn't over yet. Another huge British force landed at New Orleans, badly outnumbering a gaggle of frontiersmen led by Andrew Jackson. But their superiority made them smug and they attacked the American entrenchment head-on. It cost them two thousand of their best men compared to Jackson's loss of only seventy. Neither side should have lost any of their men, because a peace treaty ending the war had been signed in Europe two weeks earlier. Oddly, news of Jackson's rout reached the people ahead of word of the peace treaty, and even Americans who had opposed the war were thrilled to believe that one of their own had brought England to its knees once and for all. And with that burst of pride, the States were completely united for the first time. But even though it had become more important to think of oneself as an American rather than the citizen of an individual state, sectionalism was far from dead.

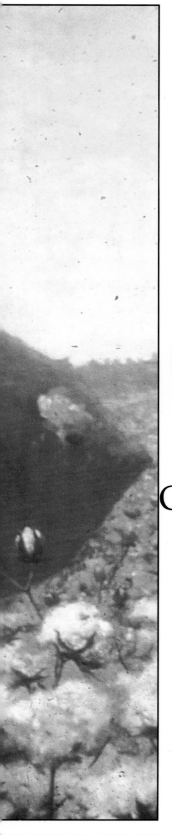

THE GATHERING CLOUD

On July 4, 1826, as America was enthusiastically celebrating the fiftieth anniversary of the Declaration of Independence, the oldest signer of the document had agreed to raise a toast to "Independence Forever" in a little New England village. But John Adams never lifted the glass. Before the day was over, the former president was dead. It was claimed that his last words were "Thomas Jefferson still survives," but he had no way of knowing that the principal writer of the Declaration had himself died a few hours earlier.

It was the end of an era, but the beginning of a dramatic new one. Immigration from Europe, which had slowed to a trickle in the years after the Revolution, grew to unbelievable proportions. The addition of new territories in the West, including Texas and California, after the Mexican War more than doubled the size of the United States, and migrating Americans filled the land in large enough numbers for the admission of more new States to the Union. The new states would eventually become the catalyst for splitting the Union apart over the issue of slavery, but in the 1820s there was a much bigger issue setting Americans at each other's throats.

After the War of 1812, the country went through a period of prosperity still remembered as the "Era of Good Feeling." It increased the power and the profits of Northern manufacturers, and planters in the South, whose own profits on cotton and rice doubled, mortgaged their land to buy more. Then, as suddenly as the good times had come, they ended, and America was plunged into the darkest depression it had ever seen. Hundreds of banks failed, and those that kept their doors open cut the money supply in half, and although they called in their loans, their debtors by and large didn't have the cash to cover them. The hardest hit were farmers, especially in the South.

The Northern factory owners were hard-pressed, too, and began lobbying Congress to take action on an idea that had been troubling Congresses from the beginning. A tariff on imported goods, they said, would encourage more native industry to everyone's benefit. The people were traditionally opposed to

the idea. They regarded manufacturers as their natural enemy, feeling that they exploited their workers and believing that their lust for profits meant higher prices and poorer quality. The opposition was especially strong in the South, whose planters and farmers relied on European markets and who had a strong fear that cutting imports would also affect exports.

The lobbyists managed to get the tariffs passed, and when they did, cracks in the Union began to widen. In South Carolina, a special convention announced that it considered the law null and void because it was, in their opinion, unconstitutional. After declaring that they wouldn't recognize any court decision on the subject, the South Carolinians said that if the Federal Government attempted to collect any tariff within their state, they would consider themselves "absolved from all further obligation to maintain or preserve their political connection with the people of the other States."

President Andrew Jackson met their secessionist manifesto with words equally tough. "Fellow citizens of my native state," he wrote, "let me not only admonish you, as the First Magistrate of our common country, not to incur the penalty of its laws, but to use the influence that a father would over his children whom he saw rushing to certain ruin." The South Carolina Legislature just smiled and incorporated the convention's proclamation into law, to which Jackson responded by going to Congress for the power to use force against his native state. He also asked for laws to reduce the tariffs, and Congress gave him what he wanted on both requests. In South Carolina, the stick was ignored and the carrot praised, as a victory for "this little state" over the giant Union. Secession had been avoided, but only for twenty-seven years.

By 1833, when Congress pulled the fangs of the tariff question, opposition to the institution of slavery, the foundation of the Southern economy, was

Above: *The Mexican War sent U.S. Marines to capture the "Halls of Montezuma."*

Facing page, left: *With the publication of his newspaper* The Liberator, *in 1831, William Lloyd Garrison was one of the first to speak out against slavery.*

Facing page, right: *It was said that Garrison inspired Nat Turner's slave rebellion that cost some sixty lives and brought fear to the South.*

beginning to become a strong political force in the North. Reformers had been talking against slavery since Colonial times, but most Americans politely ignored them until 1828, when William Lloyd Garrison wrote a powerful antislavery editorial in a Bennington, Vermont, newspaper and collected two-thousand signatures on a petition backing up his words. There had been several abortive slave uprisings over the years, but in 1831 many said that the first successful one was a direct result of Garrison's writings.

But Nat Turner, who led the revolt, said that God Himself had ordained it. The field hand said that the Spirit had appeared to him from heaven with word that Christ had laid down his yoke, and that he had been ordained to take it up and "fight against the Serpent" that was loose in the land. With the help of six fellow slaves he carefully organized his battle plan, and on the night of August 22, they led sixty others whom they had armed and provided with horses on a rampage of terror through the Virginia countryside, killing sixty-one farmers and their families. Hundreds of whites ran for their lives and, along with Federal troops sent in to put down the insurrection, butchered any slaves who crossed their path, but Nat Turner was not among them. He managed to stay out of harm's way for two months before he was finally betrayed by two black women and forced to stand trial. He was unrepentant even up to the gallows, and most Americans, who have always had a penchant for suspecting conspiracies, believed that the Turner revolt was just the tip of the iceberg and that a general revolt had begun.

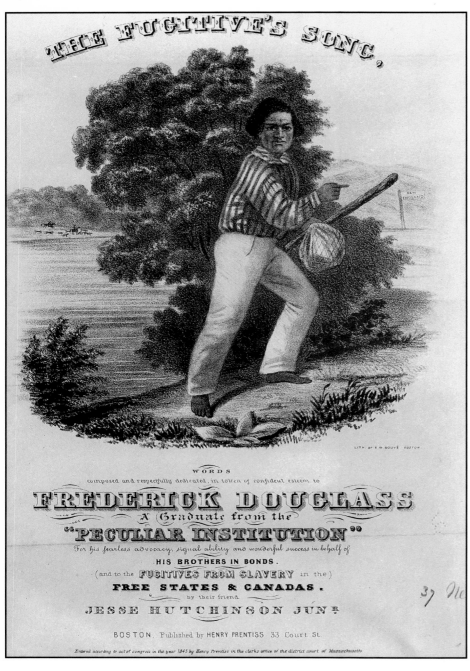

WORDS

composed and respectfully dedicated, in token of confident esteem to

FREDERICK DOUGLASS

A Graduate from the

"PECULIAR INSTITUTION"

For his fearless advocacy, signal ability and wonderful success in behalf of

HIS BROTHERS IN BONDS.

(and to the FUGITIVES FROM SLAVERY in the)

FREE STATES & CANADAS.

by their friend

JESSE HUTCHINSON JUN^r.

BOSTON. Published by HENRY PRENTISS 33 Court St.

Entered according to act of congress in the year 1845 by Henry Prentiss in the clerks office of the district court of Massachusetts

Above: *Sheet music supporting his cause helped make the ex-slave and ardent Abolitionist Frederick Douglass better-known, but many of his appearances in the North were met with violence.*

be in the right place at the right time. The country was going through a religious revival in the '30s, and there was a general feeling among Americans that they had erred and strayed from their ways like lost sheep. The businessmen who had fought for the tariff were perceived as wickedness personified, with no God but the almighty dollar. The working class was finding relief at the bottom of a whiskey bottle and drunken men were beating their wives and children and then deserting them. Women were beginning to wonder why they didn't have more control over their own lives, and men were agonizing over the way their government was treating the Indians, which was shameful. Everyone was appalled at the level of violence in the streets, the high degree of political corruption, the huge gulf between rich and poor and the possible threat to their traditional values by newcomers from abroad. And most of all, they shuddered when they heard the words "… all men are created equal" at Fourth of July celebrations, where even free blacks were denied the right to join them in their toasts to freedom. When abolitionist preachers told them that slavery was a sin in the eyes of God, they were finally ready to believe it.

On the political front, seventy-year-old former President John Quincy Adams, who was distinguishing himself in his second career as a Congressman from Massachusetts, began presenting anti-slavery petitions to the House of Representatives. His colleagues were not amused, and when he tried to introduce one instigated by the Quaker Abolitionist Lucretia Mott and signed by nearly one-hundred-and-fifty women, Southern Congressmen rose up in horror, protesting that women had no business meddling in the affairs of men. Adams said he himself had no doubt that females were citizens, but the Southerners decided that it was time to put an end to the old man's delusions and declared that Congress didn't have the power even to discuss the issue of slavery, which was one of the sacred rights of individual states. A committee confirmed it and ruled that any petitions regarding slavery should be tabled without any publication or "disquieting" discussion. The vote was nearly two to one in favor of the so-called Gag Rule, but Congressman Adams, whose father had spent his retirement writing a brilliant defense of American Constitutional Government, had another arrow in his quiver: the Constitution's First Amendment. He was generally regarded as a nuisance and hooted down whenever he rose to speak, but he never missed an opportunity. After presenting hundreds of anti-slavery petitions, he appeared in the House with a piece of paper he

In a way, it had. Garrison's newspaper, *The Liberator*, only had about fifty subscribers at the time, but in its first issue he had warned in bold capital letters, "I WILL BE HEARD!," and Turner's action provided grist for his mill. He was generally regarded as a fanatic in the North, but in the South he was routinely denounced, which is precisely why he was heard.

In spite of his brusque manner, Garrison nurtured the anti-slavery movement because he happened to

said was a petition from a group of slaves asking to have slavery abolished. The response was deafening, but without missing a beat, Congressman Adams quietly said that he wasn't offering it for debate, but simply stating he had the slaves' signatures. It only enraged the conferees even more, and they voted to censure Adams on the grounds that he was encouraging a black revolt. The debate went on for days and Adams bested his opponents. More important, the issue of slavery was part of it, along with free speech, which eventually was confirmed as a right extended even to Congressmen. But the slaves weren't free yet.

The number of anti-slavery newspapers grew to well over fifty, and their pages were filled with inspirational stories of the Underground Railroad, an organized effort to move escaped slaves from the South to the safety of Canada. It wasn't enough for the runaways to cross the Mason-Dixon Line into states that had outlawed slavery; the Supreme Court

Above: *Kansas was an early flashpoint in the anti-slavery struggle, but life went on in spite of the violence. Events such as the outdoor baptism shown here helped to bring people closer together*

had ruled in its decision on the Dred Scott case that a slave in a free state wasn't legally free. The people who risked their lives to shelter the runaways remained anonymous, but the tales of what they were doing lured thousands to the Abolitionist cause, at least in spirit. There were anti-slavery societies in every major Northern city and in many small towns, and their rallies unnerved the Southerners, who felt compelled to defend the institution of slavery no matter where they had previously stood on the issue. The rallies unnerved a lot of Northerners, too, and anti-black counter-demonstrations and riots were as common as Abolitionist meetings. Over time people became bored with the activism, and by the 1840s they were distracted by other issues they considered more important. Many were brought back to the cause through newspaper accounts of thrilling escapes among the more than thirty-thousand runaway slaves who worked their way north. And thousands were moved to tears by the flight of a girl named Eliza, who carried her baby across ice floes in the Ohio River with bloodhounds yapping at her heels; a story told by Harriet Beecher Stowe in her book *Uncle Tom's Cabin*.

But there were those who thought that rallies, novels, and even tears weren't enough. Among them was John Brown, a staunch Abolitionist who had personally delivered escaped slaves across the Canadian border and who had led battles against pro-slavery farmers in Kansas, including a foray to

Below: *In some parts of the South, plantation owners freed their own slaves long before the Civil War broke out.*

kidnap five slaves that resulted in the murder of a white man and put a price on Brown's head. But it was what was in his head that was the problem. Brown was convinced that passive resistance had been tried and failed and the time had come for action. He planned to begin a massive slave uprising in Virginia by taking over the Federal arsenal at Harpers Ferry and using the guns and ammunition stored there to arm local blacks, making them the nucleus of an army that would march southward, gathering strength by freeing slaves as it went. The raid on the arsenal was a success, and Brown's men went on to capture a nearby plantation owned by a grand-nephew of George Washington. The planter escaped, ironically with the help of his own slaves,

and the shocked residents of the town called out the militia, which managed to stop Brown's embryo army in its tracks. By the time Colonel Robert E. Lee arrived to take charge, most of Brown's men were casualties of the all-night battle and Brown himself was taken prisoner.

During his trial for treason, Brown was not only unrepentant, but used the court as a platform for ringing Abolitionist oratory, and he went to the platform of the gallows itself with his head high after having denounced "wicked, cruel and unjust" disregard of the rights of millions of slaves. It was a dramatic moment and thoughtful people, both north and south of the Mason-Dixon Line, knew that the die, at last, was cast.

Below: *Opposition to the idea that blacks should be free still lingered long after the end of the war in parts of the South.*

Facing page: *After John Brown captured the Federal Arsenal at Harpers Ferry, Virginia, to get weapons for a slave revolt, he was captured and hanged.*

Left: *In 1857, the U.S. Supreme Court ruled that although former slave Dred Scott (left) lived in a free state, he didn't have the rights of citizenship.*

Above: *With her novel* Uncle Tom's Cabin, *Harriet Beecher Stowe became the first to put the slavery issue on personal terms. It sold 300,000 copies in 1852 alone, and was adapted into a play that influenced thousands more.*

Facing page: *When their working conditions were eventually improved, women, many of whom had provided the strongest support to the anti-slavery movement, were themselves still slaves to machines and still lacked equal status with men.*

This page: *Even as they protested the institution of slavery, whole families were virtual slaves themselves in the mills and factories of the North, where children worked beside their mothers, and their fathers also put in long hours of hard work for small wages.*

Left: *The Battle of Gettysburg in Pennsylvania cost the Confederate Army 25,000 men.*

Below: *The Civil War began on April 12, 1861, when Confederate troops opened fire on Fort Sumter in Charleston.*

THE HOUSE DIVIDED

Lawmakers had been on edge during several sessions of Congress as they debated whether new States should be admitted as slave or free, but after Brown's execution, one Congressman said that among his colleagues the only ones who didn't carry a knife and a gun were the ones who carried two guns. They didn't use them, of course; most claimed they were just trying to protect themselves against the others. Besides, it was an election year.

Four years earlier a group of antislavery politicians had banded together in Illinois to form a new party calling themselves Republicans. Essentially moderates, they were opposed to slavery, but equally opposed to Abolition, and their platform called for stopping the further spread of slavery into new states. But by the time of the election of 1860, opposition to slavery all by itself was enough to set teeth on edge in the South. Abraham Lincoln, the Republican candidate, made it quite clear that he didn't think Congress had any right to interfere with slavery where it existed, that Northern States didn't have the right to block fugitive slave laws, and that violence like John Brown's raid was beneath contempt. But the South wasn't in a mood for compromise. The Republicans were against slavery and, that, as far as they were concerned, was that. They didn't have much love for the Democrats, either, and fielded one of their own to run against the regular Democratic candidate, Stephen Douglas. Then, just for good measure, they started a new party and the election became a four-way race. Lincoln polled only about a third of the popular vote, which made him a minority president, and he lost all of the Southern States. It was easily predictable. Long before the election, prominent Southern newspapers had been telling their readers that with a Republican in the White House, Abolition would surely become the law of the land, and the South itself would be enslaved by new and bigger tariffs. But there was a remedy outside the voting booth. As a Charleston editorial writer pointed out: "The Southern States can dissolve their union with the North, and Mr. Lincoln and his Abolition cohorts will have no South to reign over." It didn't matter that prominent Abolitionists had also denounced the Republican candidate. Two months after Lincoln's election, and a month before his inauguration, seven States seceded from the Union. In another three months, General Pierre Beauregard ordered his Confederate Army to attack Fort Sumter, in Charleston, and President Lincoln declared that the dreaded "insurrection" had begun.

Four more States seceded immediately, and the Confederate Government headed by President Jefferson Davis moved its Capital to Richmond, Virginia. But neither side was ready for war. Even with the addition of the Border States of Missouri, Tennessee and Kentucky, which stayed on the fence but supported the Confederacy, the South's population was only about nine million, more than a third of whom were slaves. The North was home to

Right: *Pictures of slave auctions published in the North made many aware of the "Peculiar Institution".*

Below: *George B. McClellan, who was removed when President Lincoln personally took charge of the war.*

Right: *The Union Army began the Civil War commanded by General Winfield Scott, a hero of the Mexican War.*

twenty-three million. The South had no gun factories, its farms didn't produce enough food to feed the people who worked them, let alone an army, and its transportation network was pitiful compared to the enemy's. Worse, the principle of State's Rights, which had encouraged them to withdraw from the Union in the first place, kept them apart in spite of the high-sounding ideal of confederation.

Once the call was issued for volunteers in the North, patriotism became the order of the day. Flags that had been in mothballs since the War of 1812 were hung out on front porches; little girls wore red, white and blue ribbons in their hair, and little boys played at being soldiers. Their older brothers thought that being a soldier was a form of play, too, but after the picnics that were organized to give them a proper send-off faded in their memories, they discovered they had been wrong. They wore their independence like a badge of honor and, as one of them pointed out, "we had no patience with red-tape tom-foolery." The Union Army had a discipline problem. Its officers, most of whom were raw recruits themselves, and political appointees at that, had their work cut out.

It was quite a different story in the South, where Lincoln's call for recruits was viewed by nearly everyone as a threat to their homes as well as their way of life, and volunteers poured in by the thousands to counter it. Class distinctions had never completely disappeared there, and men were used to taking orders from people higher up the social scale. It was a rare young man who wasn't an experienced horseman, and most had learned to fire a rifle long before they were nearly as tall as one. A large number of them had also been educated in military schools, and some of the most experienced officers from the U.S. Army had defected and gone home to the South.

Although the issue of slavery had driven them apart, long before either army was ready for battle that cause had faded far into the background. Though each side was willing to fight and even die for what it considered a noble cause, the men and boys who volunteered in the North believed they were defending their country, whose foundation was the Union. They believed that being united was their only sure defense against rapacious European monarchs waiting in the wings to turn them back into subservient colonies. In the South they rallied to assert their right as individuals to control their own destiny. Both causes were as traditionally American as the Declaration of Independence itself. Well over six-hundred-thousand Americans would die over the next four years, each in his own way defending the basic ideas of the Founding Fathers.

Facing page: *States began seceding from the Union as soon as Abraham Lincoln was elected president. By the time he was inaugurated, seven had left.*

Below: *It was possible to avoid serving in the Union Army by paying $300 for an exemption. In New York, protests by men too poor to avoid military service led to a bloody riot.*

Left: *Robert E. Lee led the Confederate Army following his creed that "Duty is the sublimest word in our language."*

Below: *After the battle of Shiloh, Lincoln answered calls for Grant's removal by saying, "I can't spare this man. He fights."*

Facing page: *When Ulysses S. Grant took over the Union Army, he ordered simultaneous attacks on all fronts. Losses were huge, but Grant took his own advice: "When in doubt, fight."*

Neither side anticipated what the cost might be. The Confederacy was confident from the beginning that the North would soon tire of war and that they'd then be allowed to become an independent nation. For his part, Lincoln was anxious to get the fighting over with before the end of the short enlistments of his volunteer army.

Early successes in the Border States prompted editorial writers and a large majority of the people in the North to press for an attack on Richmond, and in the summer of 1861, the Union Army, though totally unprepared, responded to the pressure and marched south from Washington, followed by a long train of civilians carrying picnic baskets to watch the fun. But there was no fun to watch when the Confederate Army led by General Thomas J. Jackson met them at Bull Run, about thirty miles down the road. Though outnumbered and outmaneuvered at first, Jackson earned his nickname "Stonewall" that day by refusing to retreat. And when Confederate reinforcements arrived, the Yanks turned and ran in panic, crashing through the ranks of picnickers behind their lines. Theoretically, the Rebels won, but they believed they had won the war and many simply went home. And it gave the Army of the Potomac the message that their enemy was something more than a confederation of stupid farm hands.

The General in charge of the Union Army at the time was Winfield Scott, a hero of the War of 1812 and of the Mexican War. He had cut a dashing figure

Above: *Lincoln's 1863 Emancipation Proclamation only freed slaves in the Confederacy, where he had no authority.*

Right: *The destruction of Richmond, Virginia, the Confederacy's capital, on April 2, 1865 – the beginning of the end of the Civil War.*

back in those days and earned the name "Old Fuss And Feathers," but by 1861, he weighed in at more than three hundred pounds and his aides had to use a block and tackle to get him on and off his horse. Even at seventy-five his mind was still sharp, and he was a master strategist, but after Bull Run Lincoln was faced with an image problem, and he put General George McClellan in charge. The image was exactly right. McClellan was a thirty-four-year-old West Point graduate, athletic and handsome, a proven leader in battle and a man with a magnetic personality. He also had an all-consuming ego and he hated to lose. To make sure that wouldn't happen, he set to work to turn his badly trained army into something worthy of his own nickname, "Young Napoleon." They drilled for weeks, the weeks turned to months, and there was no sign that he considered them ready to march on Richmond. Meanwhile, the army in the field was being mauled by the Confederates, and Jefferson Davis, himself a West Point man, was

listening to advice to go on the offensive and take the war to the North. Finally, in desperation, Lincoln said, "If McClellan does not wish to use the army, I would like to borrow it."

McClellan finally got the message and marched on the Confederate Capital over a circuitous route through Yorktown, which it took him a month to capture. Then, with Richmond in sight, he was met by an army led by Robert E. Lee and Stonewall Jackson, and he was driven back to the Chesapeake, not exactly defeated, but certainly chastened. Another Union army marched on Richmond again a few months later and was turned away by Lee at the second Battle of Bull Run. It encouraged the Confederates to cross into the North, were Lee met McClellan's army at Antietam in Maryland. Like the first Bull Run engagement, neither side could claim a clear victory. Lee was forced to retreat back into Virginia, but McClellan didn't follow, and for that he was eventually fired. But his men had given a good account of themselves at Antietam, and Lincoln used the victory as an opportunity to issue his Emancipation Proclamation. The famous document, formalized on January 1, 1863, declared that slaves in the rebellious States were forever free. He carefully avoided giving the same freedom to those held in Border States, fearing it would incite their governments to leave the Union and, of course, his power to proclaim anything that affected the Confederate States had long since been taken away. But it was a moral victory, both for him and for the Union, and two years later, after the war had ended, the individual States made Emancipation a reality by approving the Constitution's Thirteenth Amendment.

The Proclamation enraged the South, where it was generally seen as a ploy to encourage a slave uprising. It also had a negative effect on the Union Army, and hundreds of soldiers, claiming they had signed up to defend the Union and not to free slaves, headed for home. Lincoln, meanwhile, put Ambrose Burnside in command of his army, but after suffering more than twelve thousand casualties at the Battle of Fredericksburg, the General was quickly replaced by "Fighting Joe" Hooker, a West Pointer who had become a California wine-maker by the time the war broke out. He allegedly had a taste for stronger drink, and his name became synonymous with the shot glass used to measure whiskey, not to mention the women who followed the troops. Lincoln had strong reservations about his fifth commander, but in terms of esprit de corps he was a perfect choice. His men loved him and it was clear that they would

Left: *After Union forces pushed Lee's army back from Antietam Creek, Maryland, in September 1862, foreign governments abandoned plans to intervene in the American Civil War. And, as the first Union victory, the battle gave President Lincoln the opportunity to issue his Emancipation Proclamation.*

follow him anywhere. Fighting Joe led them to Chancellorsville, Virginia, where Robert E. Lee scored his greatest victory and the Army of the Potomac lost seventeen thousand men. Lee's losses were nearly as numerous, and the Confederacy lost its great general, Stonewall Jackson, to what today is known as "friendly fire," bullets from the guns of his own men. But, in spite of the blow, Lee decided to take advantage of the situation, and not long afterward the Confederate Army headed for Washington. In the face of the threat, Hooker, who had seen enough of Robert E. Lee, resigned his commission. He was replaced by George Meade,

who barely had time to get used to the idea that the destiny of the Union was in his hands when Lee's army met his in the little Pennsylvania town of Gettysburg.

The three-day Battle of Gettysburg was the bloodiest of the war, producing some fifty-one-thousand casualties. When it was over, Lee's men retreated south, and although they were trapped at the Potomac River after a bridge had been destroyed, Meade didn't attack them and they were able to escape. Lincoln was furious, but the disaster at Gettysburg ended Lee's hopes of carrying the war into the North, and there was good news from the

Below: General William T. Sherman's men destroyed cities and ripped up railroads, cutting a swath of destruction sixty miles wide as they marched through Georgia. "War is hell," said the general.

Above: *William Tecumseh Sherman was among the first to believe that wars should be taken to civilian populations as well as to armies in the field.*

Left: *Jefferson Davis of Mississippi was made president of the Confederate States of America when the Civil War broke out.*

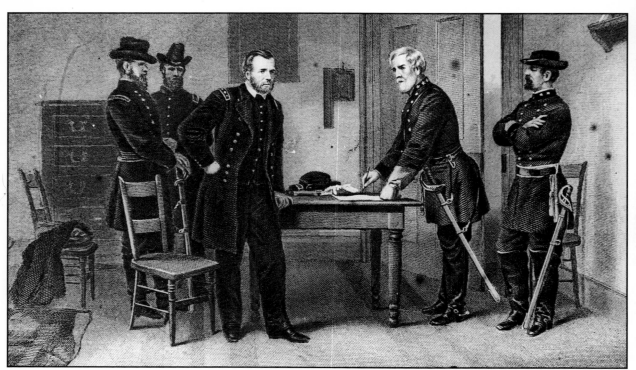

These pages: *After Lee surrendered at Appomattox Court House, Virginia, Grant told his men outside, "the Rebels are our countrymen again." But the fields nearby were littered with their dead countrymen. Within the year, a mass hanging of the conspirators in the death of President Lincoln provided another grim reminder of a national trauma that would continue for generations to come.*

West: General Ulysses S. Grant had taken Vicksburg, and the Mississippi River was in Union hands. Not long afterward, Grant moved on to Tennessee, where he scored stunning victories that swept the Volunteer State clear of Rebels and opened the way for General William T. Sherman to cut a sixty-mile-wide path through Georgia to the sea, and then north from Savannah through the Carolinas. Grant was rewarded with the title of General-in-Chief, and the following spring he headed in the direction of Richmond with one-hundred-thousand men. He lost half of them in the Virginia Wilderness, but pressed on to Cold Harbor, where in less than half an hour he lost seven thousand more. But still Grant kept on fighting. "I propose to fight it out if it takes all summer," he thundered. It took all summer and all winter, too.

By the end of 1864, the Confederacy was reduced to Virginia and the Carolinas; Grant's army was within striking distance of Richmond and reinforcements were ready to join him from deep within the South as well as from the North. Jefferson Davis called for a peace conference, but Lincoln refused unless the Confederacy would agree to rejoin the Union and free its slaves, and the war dragged on. Richmond itself fell on April 3, and five days later Lee's army was cornered at Appomattox Court House. After accepting their surrender, Grant reported to his troops: "The war is over and the Rebels are our countrymen again."

Left: *With the war's end, new invaders overran the South: the so-called carpetbaggers from the North and scalawags from the South.*

A NEW BIRTH OF FREEDOM

The post-war era is known as "Reconstruction," but to many Americans it was more destructive than the war itself. In the North, the national debt had climbed into the billions for the first time, and close to a million-and-a-half veterans had to be assimilated into the economy. The South had been pounded beyond recognition and needed to be rebuilt, but there were other problems that plagued every American. After all those years of pressure to free the slaves, more than three-and-a-half million of them, most of whom were illiterate and none of whom had any experience with the concept of earning money to take care of themselves and their families, were free at last. They became fair game for con men and swindlers, and that gave lawmakers an excuse to get tough with the South.

With the loss of President Lincoln to an assassin's bullet before the guns of war had grown cold, the Republicans found themselves without a moderate leader. They also found themselves without the dominant issue of slavery that had brought them together in the first place. Many of them were sincerely interested in promoting black equality, but the radicals among them saw the Democrats rebuilding their Southern power base and decided to even the balance by giving blacks the right to vote. President Andrew Johnson's veto of their bill, which they managed to override, led to a call for a Constitutional Amendment for black suffrage and a plan to divide the South into military districts under the iron rule of Union generals. Their demands also denied readmission to any state that didn't allow blacks to vote. The result was to give political power to "scalawags," renegade Southerners, and "carpet-baggers," opportunists from the North. Both Lincoln and Johnson had proposed gradual suffrage, giving the vote to blacks slowly as they became politically aware, and they were probably right. When unscrupulous whites manipulated the local governments by manipulating the new black voters, states already hard pressed went deeper into debt, and higher taxes destroyed nearly as many farmers as had the war. Frustrated whites put on the robes of the Ku Klux Klan to intimidate black voters and began inventing schemes to deny them their rights, and these were effective for another hundred years.

Andrew Johnson made no bones about his opposition to the radicals who had taken over his party, and when their power in Congress increased after the election of 1866, they decided to put him out of his misery. He routinely vetoed most of the laws they passed and they usually voted to override him. When it happened with a law that would forbid a president to fire one of his own appointees without Senate approval and Johnson dismissed his Secretary of War, Edwin Stanton, they thought they had him. Johnson argued that Stanton was a holdover from Lincoln's Cabinet, but Congress would have none of it and set the wheels in motion to impeach him. Fortunately for both Johnson and country, in the trial that followed the Senate acquitted the President by one vote. It clipped the wings of the radicals and, although their reconstruction policies plagued the country for generations afterward, they lost the opportunity to make matters worse. But there was another kind of opportunity waiting in the wings.

Although politicians often loom larger than life they are, after all, only human, and once having had the benefits of power, it's only natural for them to want to keep it. As the 1865 presidential election drew closer, the Republicans had already repudiated their incumbent and the voters had grown weary of their shenanigans. It could have spelled disaster, but the Democrats were, as usual, divided among themselves, and the man most Americans felt had saved the Union and could save it again was willing to take on the job.

Facing page, left: *As the railroads pushed west in the 1860s, Chinese men were imported to do the work, bringing a new ethnic group into the American melting pot.*

Below: *When President Lincoln was assassinated by actor John Wilkes Booth five days after the war ended, many in the North believed the murder had been planned by Confederate President Jefferson Davis and that Booth was a Southern hired gun.*

Ulysses S. Grant admitted that he had only voted once in his life, for James Buchanan in the 1856 election. Buchanan was a Democrat, but that didn't stop the Republicans from offering Grant their nomination in '68, nor did it stop the former general from accepting. As recently as a decade earlier, no one had ever heard of the man who at that time was living up to his boyhood nickname, "useless," as a clerk in his brother's leather store in Galena, Ohio. He had already been cashiered from the army for drunkenness, he had tried selling real estate and failed in a boom market, and he had made a mess of farming land that had been given to him. His brother regarded him as an incompetent fool, but he had to admit that Ulysses was a willing worker, even though he detested the leather business because of a deep love for the animals whose skins he was forced to handle. Even as a small boy that love had made him one of the best horse-trainers in all of Ohio, but, except for that, he didn't show much talent for anything.

When he turned sixteen it was apparent that he would never be a leather tanner and his father got him an appointment to the U.S. Military Academy at West Point. He didn't want to be soldier, either, but it was an opportunity to get out of Ohio and off he went. Grant was a disaster as a cadet. He seemed to find it offensive to brush his clothes, to button his jacket, to clean his gun or bounce out of bed at the sound of bugle call. He wasn't much of a student,

either, but at the end of his second year he was mustered out of the "Awkward Squad" and made sergeant because, it was whispered, he couldn't march in step and sergeants marched behind, not with, their men. But to Grant's credit, he graduated twenty-first in a class that had been reduced to thirty-nine out of the seventy-five who had started together four years earlier.

He was shipped off to St. Louis as a second lieutenant, then saw service in Louisiana before serving as a quartermaster under both Zachary Taylor and Winfield Scott in the Mexican War. He was among the troops that captured Mexico City and stayed there as part of the army of occupation. After that, he eventually moved to the wilds of Oregon. He had begun drinking during the war, and though he had signed several temperance pledges since then, duty in the Northwest drove him to drink again and his commanding officer drove him out of the army.

Grant had drifted back to Galena before the firing on Fort Sumter, and when Lincoln called for

Above: *The Ku Klux Klan was formed in Tennessee in 1866 with the intention of frightening blacks so they wouldn't run for office or vote in elections. Though outlawed in 1870, the Klan still exists.*

volunteers he joined the Ohio militia. The Governor wasn't at all impressed by his threadbare clothes and his slouching demeanor, but Grant was a West Point man after all, so he was assigned to the adjutant-general's office in charge of processing commissions for political appointees. His letters to the War Department asking for a better job for himself went unanswered. Eventually he gave up and went home to sit out the war, but in the meantime he had been put in charge of training the militia, and the men he turned from farm boys into soldiers were giving a good account of themselves at the front. Someone in the bureaucracy noticed and Grant was called back to take charge of the Twenty-First Illinois Regiment. He led them into Missouri, where the fighting was fierce but not glamorous enough for an officer to get himself noticed. But luck was on Colonel Grant's side, possibly for the first time in his life.

Brigadier generals were created by the president on the advice of congressmen, and when the representative from the district that included Galena suggested Grant's name to President Lincoln, the commission was approved. A few days later, Grant earned the honor and a promotion to major general with an impressive victory at Fort Donelson. He became a national hero with his triumphs at Vicksburg and Chattanooga, and after reinstating him in the regular army Lincoln made him General-in-Chief. Thirteen months later, at Appomattox, he became a hero the likes of which America hadn't seen since George Washington himself. From that day on, nothing was too good for General Grant. He was given grand houses in several cities, cash rewards in others, and everywhere he went he was treated like a member of the old aristocracy. When he was elected to the presidency with a plurality of a million-plus votes, he considered it just one more reward. Ulysses S. Grant didn't have any feel for politics and the voters loved him for it. So did the politicians. There was money to be made and it would be ever so much easier without a veto-happy president.

A company had been formed to build a railroad across the continent and the Government was committed to provide public land as well as some twenty-seven million dollars to finance the construction. To some Congressmen it was like having a key to the treasury. Many of them became stockholders in Credit Mobilier, the company that

Right: *In the 1870s, medical advances such as substituting ether for strong whiskey during surgery helped promote successful treatment.*

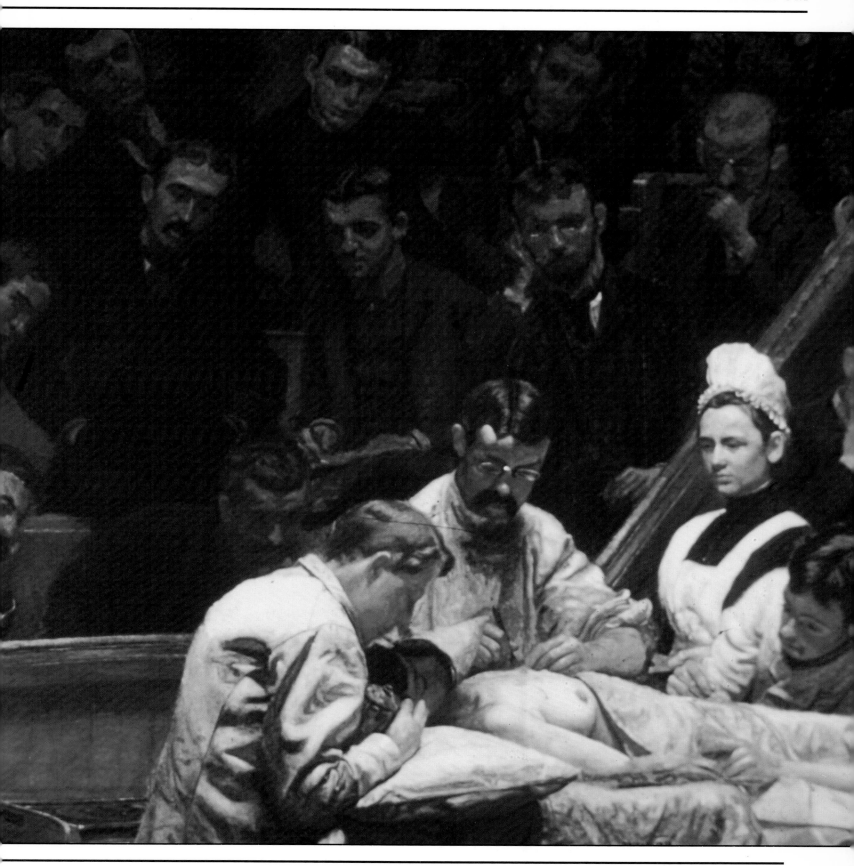

This page: *The rapid growth of the 1880s gave rise to scoundrels who were known as "robber barons." Among them were Jay Gould (above left) and his partner Jim Fisk (above right). Not content with profiteering on the Erie Railroad, they schemed to steal the government's gold reserves.*

held mortgages on the unbuilt railroad, and sat back to watch the money pour in. When their scheming came to light, they responded by closing the books and calling for an investigation which, not so surprisingly, couldn't find any proof of wrongdoing. It couldn't identify anyone in the Government who was making a profit, nor could it produce any figures, and the case was closed, even though it had been determined by other investigators that the company's stockholders had skimmed twenty-three million dollars from it and it was widely believed that most of the civil servants among them hadn't invested any of their own money. It was just as widely believed that Grant himself was totally ignorant of that scandal, and of all the others that followed during his eight-year presidency, and he probably was. Grant was unstinting in his admiration for men who could

make money, and he was very good at looking the other way when they did.

The war had created America's first real millionaires, and the so-called robber barons were manipulating the stock market and playing real-life Monopoly games with the railroads and other new industries. The rich were getting richer and officials on every level of government were not only smoothing the way but joining them on the way to the bank. Grant was indirectly involved when Jay Gould and Jim Fisk, two of the most flamboyant characters who ever walked though the doors of the Stock Exchange, tried to corner the gold market by raiding the federal supply. He cooperated with a scheme by a group of speculators to take over the island of Santo Domingo so they could control of their very own banana republic, and he never seemed to understand why the Senate wouldn't go along with the idea. Congress kept him in its hip pocket by doubling his salary, and he didn't seem at all concerned when the conferees also doubled their own and made the raise retroactive

for the previous two years. When the Treasury Department hired a strong-arm man to collect its taxes, it seemed perfectly natural to Grant to authorize him to keep half of what he collected. When his War Secretary resigned after being accused of influence-peddling, the president accepted the resignation "with deep regret." And when he discovered that his personal secretary was involved in a ring that was stealing millions in whiskey tax dollars, he wrote a letter to the court supporting the man's honor. But in spite of it all, Grant retired with his own reputation very much intact, quite possibly the most loved of any president before or since his time. Most people believed, and possibly quite rightly, that the times were to blame and not the man. The country was growing like a gangly teenager, and a few blemishes and some growing pains were to be expected.

Above: *Ulysses S. Grant, the former president, died a virtual pauper, writing his memoirs to support his wife.*

Facing page: *Daniel Boone was one of the earliest guides for westward-bound emigrants, leading the first of them across the Appalachian Mountains.*

Left: *The founder of Mormonism, Joseph Smith, led his followers into Missouri and Illinois on the way to their Promised Land in Utah.*

GONE
WEST

When the call went out for volunteers in 1804 for the Lewis and Clark Expedition, one of the first in line was Daniel Boone. At sixty-five, he was considered too old, but thanks to him and others like him the edge of civilization had already been pushed as far west as St. Louis, and some four million people were living between the Alleghenies and the Mississippi. When the Expedition started up the Missouri River, Boone was on the eastern side saluting them, passing the torch for the next great leap into the unknown.

Boone's Wilderness Road through Kentucky and Tennessee had been one of the main routes to the West until the Erie Canal connected the Hudson River with the Great Lakes, and made it easier for emigrants to move into the heartland. By the 1830s, they were ready to push beyond it. Lewis and Clark had mapped a route to Oregon and it was refined by John Jacob Astor's fur traders on their way to the Northwest. But even before the Astorians went west, Captain Zebulon Pike led a party across the prairie through Arkansas and into Colorado, where Spanish authorities arrested them and took them to Santa Fe. When they eventually made their way back to

St. Louis, traders were intrigued by the potential for profits in Spanish America and a second route to the West was established. The third major trail actually began in Palmyra, New York, a small town near the Erie Canal. A man named Joseph Smith was plowing his field there when an angel, who said his name was Moroni, introduced him to God and His Son.

"The Book of Mormon," which Smith translated from golden tablets he said the angel showed him, became the basis of whole new religion. Some people in Palmyra didn't like the idea very much and they ran Smith and his followers out of town. They had the same experience in Ohio and then in Missouri, but every time they were exiled there were more converts to follow them. They finally established a town called Nauvoo on the Mississippi River in Illinois, and before long it was the biggest city in the State. The Mormons thought they were safe at last, but Nauvoo was surrounded by "Gentiles," who weren't too neighborly or tolerant of these people who were said to practice polygamy. When Smith ordered a newspaper office destroyed because it was critical of him, the Gentiles lynched the founder of Mormonism. The mantle then fell on the shoulders of Brigham Young, who took on the job of leading his people to a new land where there would be no Gentiles. They sold their houses in Nauvoo and built wagons to make the long trip to the Promised Land, but the majority of them couldn't afford oxen to pull the wagons and were forced to pull them themselves. It was a thirteen-hundred-mile walk, but in 1847, two-thousand Mormons made the trip and the following year another three-thousand followed them. The "Promised Land" turned out to be a dry, sun-baked plain, but they put themselves in the hands of their church and together they made the valley bloom. Meanwhile, thousands of converts arrived from the East and from Europe, and before long there were enough settlers around the Great Salt Lake for Brigham Young to declare that they were an independent nation. He called it "Deseret," but the U.S. Government called it the Territory of Utah. It took them fifty years to make the idea stick.

The second great wave of westward migration was for a completely different reason. The floodgates were opened when gold was discovered in California. The Mormons had cleared the way to the Salt Lake and the Oregon Trail had taken thousands into the Northwest, but the fork in the road that led south through the mountains into California was largely avoided until 1849, when word of the gold strikes trickled back East. The Santa Fe Trail wound across deserts populated by hostile Indians, and the hundreds of miles between the end of the Mormon Trail and the Sierras were forbidding even to the Rocky Mountain trappers, who seemed quite capable of handling anything. Almost everyone contemplating the trip was told of the fate of the 1846 Donner-Reed party that was trapped in the mountains by winter snow and was nearly wiped out, but gold can make a man willing to endure anything, and in 1849 more than five thousand wagons beat a path to California over what became known as the Overland Trail. They were followed by 35,000 would-be prospectors and 60,000 head of cattle.

The cross-country trek rarely varied regardless of the intentions of the emigrants. All the trails began at Independence, Missouri, where pioneer families began arriving in early spring with all their belongings loaded into canvas-covered ox-drawn wagons. Most of them had cattle with them and usually stayed at Independence for a month or so to fatten their stock, to buy supplies and hire a mountain man to guide them, and to organize themselves into trains of about forty wagons each.

Once under way on the Oregon Trail, they found the Kansas and Nebraska countryside beautiful, though ominously quiet and desolate. Their boredom

Facing page: *After Joseph Smith's murder in 1844, Brigham Young took the Mormons across the plains to the Great Salt Lake, where they worked together to make the desert bloom.*

Below: *Many pioneer families simply banded together and went west on their own.*

Above: *Thousands went west just because it was there. And even if they didn't make it to Pike's Peak in Colorado, there was no shortage of land to settle.*

Facing page: *Thousands flocked to California in the 1849 Gold Rush, but the ones who got richest were men like Levi Strauss, who sold supplies to the gold seekers.*

was broken by sudden rainstorms that washed out their camps and swelled the rivers and streams they had to cross, but other than that the going was fairly easy until they reached Chimney Rock in Western Nebraska, where their wagon wheels began to sink into the sandy soil. They were usually out of firewood by then, and since there were no trees to cut they learned to cook over buffalo chip fires. Fort Laramie, Wyoming, offered them a chance to restock their larders and to pick up news as well as to repair their wagons and get ready for the hard part of the trip: crossing those mountains up ahead.

The trail across Wyoming and into Idaho was littered with cast-off furniture, abandoned to make the wagons less burdensome for the starving oxen. It was uphill all the way until they reached the pass that took them through the mountains, only to find even more hostile country ahead. Once they reached it they never looked back, not even the ones whose intention had been to strike it rich in the gold fields

and then go home to impress the neighbors.

The California Gold Rush lasted ten years, during which time wagon trains also carried thousands into the Oregon Territory and fortune hunters moved into the silver fields of Nevada, as well as to the gold-laced streams of Colorado and Montana. But the real rush to the West didn't begin until after 1862, when, in the midst of the Civil War, President Lincoln signed the Homestead Act. Under its terms the Government offered one hundred and sixty acres of free land to anyone who would agree to settle on it and stay there for five years to develop it into a farm. Over the following thirty years, 170 million acres were given away, adding up to an area about as big as present-day Texas. Even during the war, as General Sherman was marching across Georgia, more than seventy-five thousand marched west across the Oregon Trail. The Homestead Law had almost no restrictions. City people who had never seen a plow, let alone walked behind one, were as welcome as

These pages: *Many westward-bound pioneer families stayed on the prairie, where they built sod houses from the earth itself. They watched wagon trains passing and made friends with people like themselves who were following the American Dream. All of them were as tough as the land they conquered.*

farmers from the Confederacy and recently-arrived immigrants from abroad. The railroad companies were also given millions of acres of free land, not only for their rights-of-way, but to establish towns and farms that would provide them with customers. They mounted an advertising blitz in the Eastern States with the message, "You Need a Farm!" and thousands agreed. They carried their campaigns into Europe, and Germans, Dutch, Swedes and Danes responded enthusiastically. In Minnesota and the Dakotas the Scandinavian languages became as common as English. People were starving in Ireland; the political situation in Germany was driving people away, and by the outbreak of the Civil War about three-and-a-half million Irish and German immigrants were new American citizens, along with another million-and-a-half from other European countries. When the war was over huge numbers of them joined the families of veterans from both sides and headed west.

During the days when the only way to cross was in a wagon train, the road was hard and filled with hidden dangers, but the odds in favor of making it were quite good. In the 1840s and '50s, when about three-hundred-thousand made the trip, only about ten-thousand wound up in trailside graves, and of that number less than four hundred were victims of Indian attacks. In fact, most pioneers never even saw an Indian in the twenty weeks it took them to cover the nineteen-hundred miles. It wasn't because they weren't out there.

And when they did settle down to fence off the land and carve it up into farms, they were as likely to fall victim to the hostility of their fellow white men as to that of the Indians. As always happens to newcomers, the people already there viewed them as a threat, and in the Wild West, the cattle barons and sheepherders met the so-called sod-busters with a hostility that made the Indians seem like good neighbors.

When the Spanish arrived in the American Southwest they not only brought the first horses to North American, but they also introduced longhorn cattle from Andalusia, and long before the Anglos arrived in Texas huge rancheros were established. By the 1830s, bandits, hostile Indians and interlopers from the United States drove them all back into Mexico, and in their hurry to leave they left their livestock behind. In a few years, the herds of wild horses and cattle had learned to live and to thrive in the hostile countryside and had increased to incredible proportions.

Richard King and Mifflin Kennedy were the first to realize the value of all that beef on the hoof. But there was no way to get it to market except by walking the steers a thousand miles, and though the animals were tough, the long walk also had a tendency to make the beef tough and stringy. King and Kennedy went to work to improve the breed of both horses and longhorns and to expand their own landholdings to support even bigger herds. When the Civil War ended they were ready. The new railroads made the walk to market a good deal shorter, growing cities in the North created a new demand for beef. The soldiers who were moving out into the prairies provided a new market, too, and so did the Indians who were confined to reservations. Sportsmen were killing

buffaloes for the fun of it, and it was obvious that, unless the West was going to be populated by vegetarians, a substitute was needed. The new breed of Texas longhorn was just the ticket.

Thousands of them made the march from Texas to the railheads in Southern Kansas, and the drama of the cattle drives fired everyone's imagination. There were established farms along the route, but the ranchers just marched over them, which made the farmers very hostile, indeed. The Indians weren't too pleased, either, and there were rustlers lurking around every bend in the trail waiting for an opportunity to spook the steers and claim them as their own. But for all the danger and potential for excitement, the average cattle drive wasn't much

These pages: *The building of a railroad across the plains made the trip west much easier. Once the rails were in place cattlemen from Texas drove their steers north to load them on trains for the rest of the trip to eastern markets, and the cowboys who herded them became a romantic part of the American culture.*

Above and left: *The cowboy's life was hard. The food wasn't great and they shared their water with cows and horses. But at the end of the trail enterprising saloon-keepers made sure they could count on getting something better to drink.*

more dangerous than driving a truck on an Interstate.

About two hundred herds made the trip each year. A typical herd included about twenty-five hundred steers and a dozen cowboys to keep them moving. They took along five or six horses for each man, and the train was followed by a supply wagon driven by the most important member of the company, the cook, whose responsibility was not only to keep the coffee hot and the sourdough bread fresh, but who was also sent on ahead each afternoon to set up a camp and keep an eye peeled for danger. If there were no unusual incidents, a herd could cover about fifteen miles in a day. The average cost per steer came to about fifty cents for the whole trip, which made the cattle barons fabulously rich. If they sold their stock in Texas, the price was three dollars a head. Up in Kansas, the same animal fetched twenty dollars and, considering it cost two dollars to raise them in the first place, it was worth the effort.

The most common route they followed was the old Chisholm Trail that had been established by Jesse Chisholm, a Cherokee who supplied beef for the Army posts out on the plains. It began at the Red River and stretched north to Abilene, the town the cowboys made famous. When the cowpunchers arrived there, they collected their pay of about thirty dollars for each month they had been on the trail. It was all the money in the world to them, and there

were many ways to spend it in Abilene. There were plenty of saloons, and most of the cowboys were very thirsty after swallowing dust all the way from Texas. And if they needed to let off a little steam, it was easy to get into a brawl. Most cowboys had roots in the deep South and many of them rode the cattle drives dressed in the uniforms that had been issued to them by the Confederate Army. The Abilene City Fathers made it a point to hire marshals and sheriffs who had seen service in the Union Army, and it wasn't at all uncommon for the Civil War to be refought night after night on the streets of Abilene.

But before the fun began there was other business to attend to. A cowboy's first stop was a barber shop for a haircut and a beard trim. Next he went to a clothing store. Even in those days, no jeans would serve their needs like those made in San Francisco by Levi Strauss. Each new hat had to be imported from New York and the label inside had to say "Stetson." The boots had to have stars tooled into the leather or there was no sale, these men were Texans, after all. No store in town could hope to stay in business if the owner didn't keep up with the fashion trends that these men knew all about, even though they had been out of contact with any world but their own for three months or more.

The round of saloons and dance halls, gambling dens and bawdy houses that began once the cowboys

were properly duded-up didn't last more than a few days and, depending on the skill of the gamblers, sometimes a lot less. Once their money was gone the cowpokes drifted back to Texas, where the whole process started over again the following spring. In the meantime, they were broke and needed little jobs to tide them over. There wasn't anything they wouldn't do, but most of them spent the winter just hanging out and hanging on, bragging about their adventures on cattle drives and counting the days until they could join another.

The shortage of lawmen in the West made it customary for men to take the law into their own hands, and the legend of the American cowboy is filled with yarns about tough hombres defending their steers with blazing six-guns. But it was a rare cowboy who carried a gun. A hard and fast rule in the West made it a hanging offense to kill an unarmed man, and the cattle barons decided that their men would be safer without guns. They may have been right. In Kansas in 1873, the year the railroad reached Dodge City, twenty-five men were gunned down, but only one of them was a cowboy, and he was considered an innocent bystander.

But if cowboys were subject to gun control, the six-shooter is still considered the gun that won the West. The man who invented it was Samuel Colt, who had done a good deal of traveling with a medicine

Above: *If you broke the bank in 19th-century Las Vegas, Nevada, you'd get $10,000. Things have changed since then; you can get that much from a slot machine these days.*

Facing page: *Be it ever so humble, there's no place like home. A log cabin in the West signaled a new start and a new lease on life for pioneer families.*

Above: *The only problem for pioneers was picking the right spot to settle down. But there was plenty of wide-open country to choose from.*

131

Facing page: *Be it ever so humble, there's no place like home. A log cabin in the West signaled a new start and a new lease on life for pioneer families.*

Above: *The only problem for pioneers was picking the right spot to settle down. But there was plenty of wide-open country to choose from.*

show built around demonstrations of laughing gas. While his customers were giggling, he was turning over an idea for a pistol that could fire six bullets without reloading. His dream was to become a defense contractor, and he made a fancy model of his gun for President Andrew Jackson. If Jackson was impressed, his War Department wasn't, and Colt's market was limited to collectors. But Colt was a good salesman, and when he took his idea to the Republic of Texas, he found his mark in the person of Captain Jack Hays of the Texas Rangers.

The Rangers had their hands full fighting Indians and they were at a serious disadvantage. Each Ranger carried a rifle, a shotgun and a single-shot pistol, which required them to fight on foot against red men who used bows and arrows, but fought from the backs of horses. Captain Jack turned the tide with Colt's invention, but if he frightened the Indians with his new ability to keep firing without reloading, the six-gun wasn't very deadly. It had a small bore, it was too light, and it was badly balanced, and after firing its six bullets it needed to be taken apart before it could be reloaded. Colt went back to his drawing board in Paterson, New Jersey, and he took Ranger Captain Samuel Walker with him. Together they produced a new and improved six-gun, which became known as the Walker-Colt. In the years that followed it became standard equipment, not only for the Texas Rangers but for other lawmen and outlaws alike. It was responsible for killing more men than any handgun ever made, but in the end it earned a reputation as the gun that won the West.

Right: *The West attracted its share of colorful people, including Annie Oakley, called "Little Miss Sure Shot" by Chief Sitting Bull.*

Facing page: *Not everyone appeared on the new frontier ready for building a new life. Instead, some chose to join Annie Oakley in Wild West shows.*

THE NATIVE AMERICANS

Facing page: Once the Spanish brought horses to America, the Plains Indians had a better way to hunt bison. Their ancestors had hunted on foot, driving the huge creatures over cliffsides to kill them.

Awondrous thing happened on April 22, 1889. A month shy of the thirteenth anniversary of the Homestead Law, the Government decreed that the Territory of Oklahoma came under its terms, and before noon that day almost two-million acres were claimed. Before the sun set, the cities of Guthrie and Oklahoma City were open for business. The only problem was that up until that day Oklahoma was known as "Indian Territory," and had been off-limits to whites. The Creeks and Seminoles were paid for the land that was to be converted into farms and cities, and four years later another deal was struck with the Cherokees to allow another hundred-thousand whites to take over their Oklahoma lands in a single day. But they themselves, along with the Choctaw and Chickasaw, were relative newcomers. They had been given the land under the terms of a law passed in 1830 that forced them to trade their ancestral homes for a new life in the West where, presumably, they would stay forever out of sight and out of mind.

The Indian problem had plagued Americans from the earliest times. Prejudice and fear had a lot to do with it, but at the root of every tale of treaties broken, of farms destroyed, of Indian villages burned out of existence, was the land itself. In general, most colonists agreed with an early court decision that the natives held title to their land, but only if they were using it. To the European mind, that meant a house, a village or a farm, all of which were easy to eliminate. It was a losing proposition for the Indians, but they managed to keep their pride, and some of their territory, by fighting back. They also fought among themselves, and over time many of the tribes were forced by their own people to move westward, where they joined with their new neighbors and the French against the

British authorities on one hand and the English colonists on the other. But when the French were driven out of Canada and the Midwest at the end of the French and Indian War, the Indians were left behind to pick up the pieces, and the British authorities let them know they'd be no help. All gifts, an institution from the start, were cut off; the Indian trappers were paid less for their furs, and the English commandant ordered them to surrender their trophies of war, which often included captives who had become their wives and the mothers of their children. The policy led to a fearsome uprising by the Ottawa Chief Pontiac that left two thousand casualties among the whites on Great Lakes frontier, the first in a series of such bloodbaths that lasted through the establishment of the American nation and far beyond.

The Administrations of both George Washington and John Adams wrestled with the problem. Washington's solution was one that had always been running like a thread through most discussions since the establishment of Jamestown: to assimilate the Indians into the white man's society by making farmers of them. It was ironic that many of the crops and the methods of growing them had been introduced to the Europeans by the Indians, but not all Indians were farmers, and even if any of them might have agreed to become one, Congress turned a deaf ear to the President's idea. It was Thomas Jefferson who came up with what might be considered the final solution. Not long after the Louisiana Purchase, he had the bright idea of persuading the Indians east of the Mississippi to trade their land for tracts west of the river. He managed to translate the idea into law, and he convinced many of the tribes that their old hunting grounds were shy of game anyway and that they'd be better off out in the wide-open spaces of the West. Among the holdouts were the Cherokee of Georgia, who were already assimilated into the white man's culture and said they'd rather become citizens and stay where they were.

Meanwhile, up in the Indiana Territory, Governor William Henry Harrison was removing tribes with threats and coercion, always careful to stay on the edge of legality if not friendliness. The Shawnee Chief; Tecumseh, and his brother, who was known as The Prophet, decided their claim was as good as Harrison's, and they began visiting tribes up and down the frontier with the message that the land belonged to all Indians and no individual chief had the right to give away any of it. Harrison responded with what he characterized as a preventive war, which was eventually overshadowed by the War of

Facing page: *Sitting Bull was considered a powerful medicine man among the Sioux of the northern plains.*

Below: *Treaties with the Western tribes weren't always as honorable as the one William Penn had forged when he established his Pennsylvania colony.*

1812 and which put the Indians of the old Northwest on the side of the British. The English agents assured the Indians that the war was being fought for their benefit, and that together they would restore the old tribal lands, but the treaty that ended the war barely mentioned the Native Americans, and when the British marched home for the last time the Indians were at the mercy of the New Americans.

By 1830, all the Eastern tribes had been removed by a combination of threats, bribery and force, and only the Cherokees and the Seminoles still resisted. The Georgia State Government found the Cherokee problem especially galling because the Indians, who had a written language, had drafted their own constitution as a sovereign nation. Matters came to a head when gold was discovered within their borders and the Cherokees called on Washington to send in troops to protect them from the prospectors. President Andrew Jackson, who made no bones about his conviction that the only good Indian was a dead Indian, denied their request and encouraged the Georgians to stand up for their own rights. The Cherokees saw the handwriting on the wall and agreed to go west, but three years later three-quarters of them were still in Georgia, and Federal troops had to be sent in to move them out by force. Some managed to escape into the mountains of North Carolina, but the majority were herded westward over what they called "The Trail of Tears." Four thousand didn't survive the trip.

The Seminoles also signed a removal treaty, but as the day approached for them to trade their homes in Florida for new ones in Oklahoma, they vanished into the Everglades. The war to flush them out lasted seven years and cost the Americans fifteen hundred men. It ended when the Americans violated a flag of truce and captured their leader, Osceola, who had outfoxed thousands of professional soldiers, as well as mercenaries from other tribes and even bloodhounds. Most of his followers bowed to the inevitable and moved on, but hundreds stayed hidden in the swamps and, though the fighting stopped, they never signed a peace treaty and technically the war is still going on …. Either that, or the United States Army lost. You can take your pick.

Even the most compliant tribes were treated miserably as the whites followed them west. Some were moved a half-dozen times to get them out of the way of progress, but the people moving in behind them weren't their only problem. The planners hadn't given much thought to the tribes already living in the West who, as it turned out, weren't too pleased to share their hunting grounds with a hundred thousand newcomers. The Plains Indians had originally been farmers and fishermen before the Spanish gave them horses and completely changed their way of life, but by the time the Eastern tribes began arriving in their midst they had rewritten their own histories and completely denied that they had ever been anything but far-ranging nomads and expert horsemen. The Easterners, usually at the urging of the Great White Father, tried to scratch out farms, which to the Plains tribes was work suitable only for women, children and cowards. But the newcomers were anything but cowardly and they had better weapons, even if they were relative strangers to

Left: *Indian braves dragged their wounded away so they wouldn't be humiliated by being taken prisoner by the enemy.*

Above: *After the Sioux were defeated, Sitting Bull toured the world in full regalia as a star of Buffalo Bill's Wild West Show.*

horses. Fighting among them raged for more than forty years until the white man's wagon trains gave them all something new to think about.

They had been talked out of harassing emigrants on the Oregon and Santa Fe Trails, but as new trails began criss-crossing their hunting grounds and they were faced with starvation, the red men began to wonder if this huge land was big enough for both races. The whites had already decided it wasn't and the first blow was struck in 1854, when a small cavalry party marched on a Sioux village to settle a dispute over a stolen cow. Three villagers were shot, and the braves responded by killing all thirty of the horse soldiers. A week later troopers marched on a different Sioux village and avenged their comrades' death by killing every man, woman and child they found there. Before long all the tribes from the Desert Southwest to the Pacific Northwest were on the warpath. Treaties relegated most of

them to reservations by the mid-1860s, but the fire wasn't out yet.

When the Mexican War added the Arizona Territory to the United States, it also added the Apaches to the list of tribes that had to be dealt with. The leader of the Chiricahua Apache, Cochise, decided from the start that it would be futile to take on the United States Cavalry, but that he and his people could thrive by selling beef to wagon trains on the Santa Fe Trail. They stole the cattle from ranches in Mexico, but the Americans didn't mind and for twenty years the emigrants were well-fed and the Chiricahua prospered. Then one day in 1866 a white boy was kidnapped and Cochise was called in for interrogation. It was a one-sided discussion with the lieutenant in charge accusing the chief of lying when he said he knew nothing of the boy's fate. It happened that Cochise had brought along his wife and son, his brother and two nephews, and the lieutenant told him that all of them were his prisoners until the boy was returned to his family. Cochise drew his knife, cut a hole in the tent and escaped, but his family was restrained from following and the chief responded by holding up a stagecoach to take its passengers as hostages to exchange for them. Official records of the event have conveniently been lost, but Cochise's family was either hanged or spirited away and the hostages were murdered.

The Chiricahua were merciless after that, and hundreds of ranchers and their families were tortured to death over the next five years. By the time word of what was happening reached President Grant nearly every ranch in the Arizona Territory was abandoned and the towns virtually deserted, in spite of the fact that they were under the protection of the U.S. Army and Cochise rarely had more than one hundred braves following him. Grant's solution was to move the Chiricahua to the already-established Apache reservation west of the mountains, but when Cochise refused to move, a compromise was struck to allow them to stay where they were after they promised to obey the rules of reservation life. When Congress rejected the idea, Cochise was on the warpath again, and this time he had the support of all the Apache tribes and his army grew to ten times its former size. No white man anywhere in the Southwest was safe from them until Congress reconsidered its decision.

Cochise kept his word and peace returned, but when he died the Government broke its word and herded the Chiricahua away from their ancestral lands. The Apache responded by going to war again, and they terrorized the Southwest for another fifteen years. When their chief Geronimo finally surrendered, there were five thousand troops in the field against his thirty-six warriors, but that isn't why they surrendered. The Great White Father had secretly changed the law to allow his troops to follow

Below: *As the whites began claiming the West, Indian villages were relocated, often more than once, and frequently by force.*

Geronimo into Mexico, which up until then had been a safe haven, and with no place to run, the Apaches simply decided that discretion was the better part of valor.

To all intents and purposes the Indian Wars were over, but a dramatic climax was building in the Dakota Territory. The Cheyenne and the Sioux were assigned to reservations in the Black Hills, which had always been sacred ground to them. But rumors were spreading that the territory was rich in gold and silver, and prospectors naturally had to go in to find out if they were true. When a reporter visited there and wrote that there was enough gold in the hills to retire the national debt, the Government sent in its agents to negotiate another treaty. Their offer of six million dollars for the mineral rights was rejected, and the Indian agents suddenly became forgetful about the terms of earlier treaties that promised to provide the Indians with food and supplies. Militants led by Crazy Horse and Sitting Bull met the problem by moving their followers off the reservation into the Yellowstone Basin, where the hunting was still good, and defied the whites to do anything about it.

One unit of the army that responded, led by Colonel George Armstrong Custer, who had earned the brevet rank of general in the Civil War and was intent on earning the honor again, moved on its own, and contrary to orders, against a Sioux encampment on the Little Bighorn River. After a skirmish that sent some of the Indians running, Custer assumed he was witnessing a rout and assembled his main force to march on the village for his moment of glory. But as soon as they were out in the open, thousands of Indians rushed over the ridges and in a matter of minutes every white soldier was dead.

The army responded with a massive effort to make sure that the Indians were put in their place once and for all, and in the months that followed the Western tribes were systematically defeated. Crazy Horse was taken prisoner and murdered, and Sitting Bull led his people to the safety of Canada. He eventually returned as the star of Buffalo Bill's Wild West show and became the most famous Indian of them all. But in the meantime, back east of the Mississippi, Americans had other things on their mind. They were all invited to a birthday party.

Above: *Eventually, Indian hunting grounds were fenced off and soon, thanks to the efficiency of the white man's guns, there were no bison left to hunt.*

Left: *Wagon trains were only occasional targets of war parties, thanks to early treaties. But the possibility added a note of terror to journeys.*

Above: *"The Boy General," George Armstrong Custer, faced the wrath of the Sioux nation in 1876 at the Little Bighorn River.*

CENTENNIAL SUMMER

Landmark anniversaries are usually marked by backward glances, but the hundredth anniversary of America's Declaration of Independence was never conceived as a nostalgia trip. It may have been because the country's recent history had been relatively traumatic; it could have been that the celebration was held in Philadelphia, where reminders of the Spirit of '76 were around every corner; but it probably was America's fascination with the future that made the Centennial Exposition one of the great turning points of our own past.

The party in Fairmount Park was two years in the making, in a space that had been admirably landscaped only a few years earlier but was completely altered for the Centennial. About 20,000 trees and shrubs were planted, along with more than one-hundred-and-fifty-three acres of lawns and flower beds. Miles of streets and sidewalks and railroad tracks wound among them, over bridges and past fountains, to give access to more than two-hundred-and-fifty new buildings, each and every one acclaimed as a palace.

It was all finished by May 2, 1876, when President Grant arrived to declare the Fair officially open. After listening to a special march written for the day by the German composer Richard Wagner, and

Left: *Fairmount Park, it was said, was "the most beautiful place in the whole civilized world." Nature was improved upon with the planting of 20,000 trees and shrubs and 153 acres of lawns and gardens.*

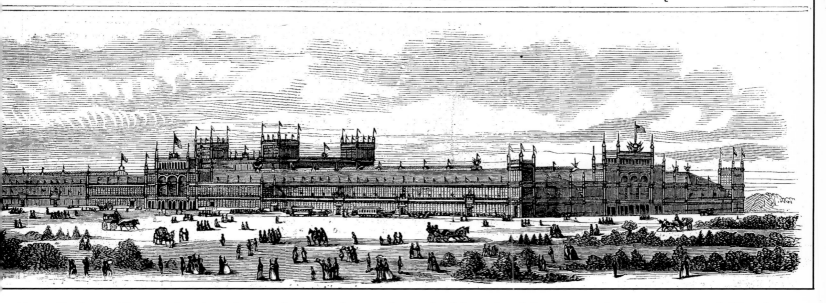

Above: *The Centennial's Main Exhibition Building was the focal point of the celebration.*

Below: *All the individual states were represented in the Agricultural Building.*

hearing a hymn whose words were the work of the American poet John Greenleaf Whittier, the President made a brief speech and, as the crowd roared, a massed choir burst into a spirited rendition of Handel's "Hallelujah Chorus." As they sang, American flags were hoisted on one hundred flag poles, and when they finished, cannon across the river fired a hundred-gun salute as thirteen replicas of the Liberty Bell were tolled in unison one hundred times. Then, as the band played "Hail Columbia," the popular choice to become the country's national anthem, the President led four thousand dignitaries into the main building for what was for all of them the main event of the day.

There in the center of the room was the biggest machine built up to that time. It was a seven-hundred-ton steam engine built by engineer George Corliss to provide the power for all the hundreds of other machines that were displayed throughout the building. Its two huge, silver-plated cylinders drove a thirty-six-foot flywheel that delivered 2,520 horsepower. The industrialists in the audience were moved to tears; the farmers, many of whom were still using the power of a single horse to plow their fields, couldn't stop cheering.

There were steam engines of every description on the fairgrounds, as well as the railroad locomotives which had become tangible symbols of freedom to most Americans by then. But there was something new: machines their promoters said would end forever the country's dependence on coal and wood because they were run by something called "internal combustion," and used some stuff called petroleum

that folks were at that very moment drilling from the ground out near Pittsburgh. Well, maybe. Fairgoers decided to reserve judgement on that one. They were just as sceptical about a machine a brewer said cooled his beer with electricity instead of ice, but after a frosty brew or two they were ready to accept the idea. What they couldn't swallow, though, was the prediction that this same machine would one day replace their iceboxes. And what nobody even dared to suggest was that eventually the technology would cool their buildings through the hottest of summers. There had to be something left undone for the next generation, after all.

It would have been hard to convince anyone that air-conditioning would come along to make movie theaters more comfortable. Movies were in the future, too, but in 1876 everyone had already seen still pictures. Photographers had been tramping all over the country for thirty-seven years, recording great events from inaugurations to hangings, and small events from weddings to nervous kids on ponies. But it was a game played by professionals only, and usually only those with the strength and determination to lug impossibly heavy equipment on their backs. Now, though, manufacturers were showing cameras small enough to carry in your pocket. They were outlandishly expensive because they were finished in rare woods and trimmed in ivory and ebony, but the technology was there and it didn't take much imagination to realize that the day was at hand when the average grandmother would have a handbag full of snapshots of her above-average grandchildren.

First, of course, drugstores had to get into the photofinishing business, but for the moment the Great Fair was giving them other things to think about. One firm introduced sugar-coated pills, and another was demonstrating gelatin capsules. A third proudly displayed a pyramid of pure, unadulterated morphine. In the same pavilion, an inventor smiled broadly through false teeth made of porcelain, which he claimed would "disarm suspicion as to their artificial nature."

Those who who still had their own teeth were able to pick them clean with the world's first toothpicks, possibly after devouring a brand-new snack called an ice cream cone. They could do it on a streetcar if they wanted to. Tracks had been laid over Philadelphia's cobblestoned streets and around the fairgrounds to give fairgoers the smoothest ride imaginable. As the official guide book pointed out: "If you wish to view the entire square-toed metropolis without the trouble of walking, jump into a street car … and interview a great city in a sitting posture." But the real fun wasn't in the city, it was out in Fairmount Park. And not all of it was related to the industrial future.

Visitors to the Women's Pavilion were discovering that the female sex was about to have its day. As one of them wrote home: "Some individuals want to extend women's rights to unnatural and insane extremes." But he seems to have absorbed another message, too, and added: "It is unmistakable that the application of this great principle has importantly contributed to the development of the nation." Indeed it had. There, along with a pair of napkins hand-embroidered by Queen Victoria, was a machine invented by a woman to take the drudgery out of washday. And in a nearby building, a device called a "literary piano" pointed the way out of household drudgery for many women. Anyone could see that the typewriter would change the business world, but most felt that operating one would have to be women's work because the keys were too close together for a man's hammy hands. To be sure, the most popular women's exhibit was a sculpture made of butter that stood unrefrigerated for the run of the Fair. It attracted infinitely more attention than the device Alexander Graham Bell had brought down from Boston. He said it would make it possible for people in Boston to talk to Philadelphians without ever leaving home. But even people who were familiar with clattering telegraphs didn't believe him, and Mr. Bell packed up his telephone and went home before the Fair ended.

The Exposition ran from May through November, during which time more than eight million people paid the fifty cents admission charge to be impressed by America's future. When it closed, with the touch of a telegraph key that sent an impulse from Washington to stop the great Corliss Engine, the exhibits were removed and the buildings torn down. Forty-two freight cars were needed to carry the wonders off to Washington, where they are still impressing visitors to the Smithsonian Institution. The trees and shrubs were moved to nearby Longwood Gardens, and the Corliss Engine went to Chicago to a new job in the Pullman Railway Car factory. One of the most popular exhibits, a statue of an arm holding a huge torch, known as "The Statue of Independence," was shipped to New York, where it eventually joined the rest of the figure and was placed in the harbor as the Statue of Liberty.

Even Americans who missed the Fair didn't miss the feeling of pride that overtook the country that Centennial Summer. Until then they had really never lost their European roots, and they generally looked upon the Old Country the way children regard their parents, but the Fair made them take a good look at themselves and they liked very much what they

Bottom left and below:
Bicycles were a big attraction at the Fair, but the stunner was the mighty Corliss steam engine, capable of delivering the power of 2,500 horses. It was the biggest machine that had been built up to that time.

saw. They weren't unsophisticated colonials any longer. And in Europe the feeling was mutual. Newspapers and magazines began describing Americans with words like "bold … powerful … energetic … modern … big," and, most of all, "progressive." *The Times* of London summed it all up by saying: "The New Englander [sic] mechanizes as an old Greek sculptured, as the Venetian painted or the modern Italian sings. A school has grown up whose dominant quality, curiously intense, widespread and daring, is mechanical imagination." The Industrial Revolution may have changed their world, but in America it was more than change, it was an art form.

Right and below: *The Chinese preferred to display manpower in their exhibit, but it was giant gear cutters and other steam-powered machines that stole the show.*

THE GILDED AGE

Attendance at the Centennial Exposition wasn't limited to Easterners and European journalists. After 1869, when the Central Pacific Railroad linked up with the Union Pacific at Ogden, Utah, it was possible to bounce from coast to coast on a train, and the Centennial gave many a Californian the perfect excuse to experience the adventure. By the turn of the century there were five different transcontinental routes, and it was a rare Western state that didn't have a half-dozen or more lines running through it. The competition was fierce, and about a quarter of the railroads had long since gone into bankruptcy, although the courts were generous in retaining their former directors as receivers. The great railroad man, William H. Vanderbilt, explained why when he pointed out that "railroads are not run for the benefit of the dear public ... they are built for men who invest their money." The catch was that most of the money they invested wasn't theirs. They routinely floated shares of "watered stock," collecting two or three times the amount of cash their assets could cover, and the Government was ready, even anxious, to help them get even more.

When the Union Pacific was planned, the authorities agreed to give the developers twenty square miles of free land for every mile of track they

completed, along with loans from the public treasury of sixteen thousand dollars for every mile of flat land they crossed and up to fifty thousand for each mile of track that crossed mountains. The Eastern investors who pushed west were more experienced at skimming profits, but the four men who organized the Central Pacific in San Francisco, though comparative neophytes, found themselves richer by twenty-three million dollars before the first train chugged across their line. The age of the tycoon had arrived.

The railroads created more than just a few millionaires, of course. The country got a return on its investment with the creation of new cities and towns and jobs for its citizens. They made it possible for farms to exist in areas far removed from their markets. And they opened the way to making it profitable to tap into the continent's incredible store of resources. Men whose grandfathers had dreamed of finding gold found that they could get just as excited, and possibly richer, over the discovery of a vein of coal or iron. And with those discoveries came even more opportunities. And more tycoons.

In those days, young boys were avid readers of small novels about men like Buffalo Bill who were taming the Wild West. They especially enjoyed stories of the exploits of Jesse James, who entered the American legend when he and his brother, Frank, along with the four Younger brothers, wrecked a train in Iowa and robbed all the passengers. Most ordinary people were fed up with the high-handed tactics of the railroad operators and all train robbers were heroes to them, but what made the James boys a cut above the others was the bombing of their home by railroad police that killed their brother and left their mother without an arm. Jesse himself secured a kind of immortality when he was shot in the back for a cash reward offered by the railroads by a man described as a dirty little coward with pimples and bad teeth. But the tycoons everybody loved to hate had their champion in boy's books, too. He was

This page: *The late 19th century was an era when America's heroes ranged from the outlaw Jesse James (above left) to steel magnate Andrew Carnegie (above).*

Horatio Alger, whose stories were so predictable that the average American kid could describe the plot by just reading the author's name on the title page. But they read them anyway, and they were inspired by them because, if the mood in their households was hate for the robber barons, everyone secretly hoped their son would grow up to be one. And in the America of the 1880s, it seemed easily possible.

Typical of a Horatio Alger tale was the real-life story of Andrew Carnegie. Alger preached that a lad must start at the bottom, work hard, follow the rules unquestioningly, cheerfully earn more for his employer than he was being paid himself, and save his money. When Carnegie arrived from Scotland as a teenager, he took a job in a textile mill for $1.50 a week and, by following all the rules, he rose in about ten years to a middle-management job with the Pennsylvania Railroad at nearly fifty dollars a week. It was a comfortable salary in those days, but young Carnegie had also built a cushion for himself. He invested most of his salary in iron foundries, and the building of the railroads had ballooned his return to nearly fifty-thousand dollars a year. At the time Carnegie was accumulating his nest egg, Bill Kelly, an iron maker in the hills of Kentucky, was fooling around with an idea of super-heating iron to burn away the impurities and make it into something stronger. He was generally regarded as a crackpot, and so was Sir Henry Bessemer, who had developed

Below: Men who worked in factories turning out items such as pianos dreamed of the day when they'd own the place. Or at least be able to afford a piano.

a furnace in England that could provide the required heat. Neither of them was able to translate the idea into something profitable until Carnegie saw the future in it and built Pittsburgh's first steel mill. It was an investment that changed the whole American economy, not to mention Carnegie's life. He doubled his money in a year or so, and that was only the tip of the iceberg. But fate had a little something to do with it. At about the same time Carnegie saw his first Bessemer furnace in 1872, he bought a farm for forty-thousand dollars, and saw its value grow to five million in less than a year when oil was discovered in the middle of the pasture.

He might have become a titan of the petroleum business, and given John D. Rockefeller a run for his money, if he hadn't decided to go into the steel business instead. But as it turned out, it was his company, eventually sold to J.P. Morgan and restructured as United States Steel, that became the country's first billion-dollar enterprise, all by itself worth more than the gross national product of the entire country less than a hundred years earlier. By then, at the beginning of the twentieth century, the industrial output of the United States was already far ahead of all the industrial nations of Europe combined.

Above: *When workers stood up for their rights in the early days of the labor movement, the National Guard sometimes appeared to put them down.*

But in the go-go 1890s, ninety percent of the wealth was controlled by less than ten percent of the population, and although the man in the street was noticeably better off than has father had been, there was plenty of poverty to go around, too. The working classes were beginning to organize themselves for a better break, but in spite of horrible examples of labor violence, management was capable of violence, too, and was able to keep the unions down. Ironically, the American Dream had a lot to do with it. When workers began organizing themselves into unions, the majority of Americans thought they were making a terrible mistake. When a man complained about

working in a Carnegie mill for a dollar a day, his neighbors were prone to point out that Carnegie himself had once worked for a whole week to earn not much more than that. The unions would eventually have their day, but in the meantime the age belonged to the super rich, and they didn't miss an opportunity to flaunt it.

Carnegie lived in Pittsburgh and Rockefeller in Cleveland, but the place to watch the rich at play in the Gilded Age was New York, where making money had been a municipal passion since it was known as New Amsterdam. It was not insignificant that New York had the world's first department store, created

Above: *When the rich turned to faro games to improve their income, police often arrived to save them from the gambling habit.*

in the 1850s by A.T. Stewart, an Irish immigrant who, naturally, became a millionaire many times over with an enterprise that catered to the whims and wishes of women who suddenly realized they were, as they say, born to shop. But, by the 1890s, although the cash registers at Stewart's Marble Palace were still ringing like the bells of a cathedral on Easter Day, his imported linens and laces, cashmeres and silks were becoming a bit too common for ladies who wanted to make an uncommon statement. Obviously it was necessary to import one's own, and since steamships had reduced the run from Europe to about ten days it was easily possible for anyone who could afford it to be on the cutting edge of Paris fashion well ahead of Mr. Stewart's customers.

The men who helped them do it estimated that a young woman simply couldn't scrape though the social season without at least three hundred new additions to her wardrobe, ranging from hand-painted fans, color-coordinated hairnets and gold card cases, to cloaks that complemented the fifty gowns necessary to be the belle of every ball. The balls themselves made it necessary to build finer mansions and to fill them with art that could compete with the elegance of the invited guests. All of it took lots of money, but that was the point.

The balls had a fairy tale quality about them that would have put royalty to shame, and the palaces were calculated to make crowned heads bow in frustration. After a French aristocrat visited New York he said he could never take his wife to the Tuileries again because the apartments there were "small, wretched holes … compared to what I have just seen." For New York society, there could be no higher praise. From food to fashion to the art of decoration, the only possible measure of perfection had to be French, at least as far as the women were concerned. The men of the Gilded Age tended to be Anglophiles. Most found relief from the endless task of making money by losing some of it over a few hands of whist in the card room of a private club, where they were mercifully free from female

Below: *All through the '80s and '90s the parties never seemed to end.*

conversation, which mostly centered around parties and balls, idle gossip and the politics of status. In the matriarchal society of the 1890s, the clubs gave men the kind of sanctuary they couldn't find at home. Many had been formed to bring men of similar backgrounds and professions together, but most had rules against the discussion of business matters that were as iron-clad as the rules against women. Instead, they chose to talk about horses and dogs, hunting and fishing techniques, and other activities more suitable to leisured English country gentlemen than city-bound Americans who worked six days a week even though they didn't seem to need the money.

What leisure time they had was spent at polo matches, fox hunts, yachting competitions, fly fishing, hiding behind duck blinds and, when they could afford the time, weekends with their families at their summer places in Newport, the Adirondacks or up on the coast of Maine. But when they were left to their own devices in the city they made an impression

every bit as powerful as that of their wives' soirees and balls, although on another segment of society.

It all started when millionaire Leonard Jerome ordered a fancy four-horse coach and taught himself four-in-hand driving. He trained his horses to cut capers and rear as he sat behind them, with a whole bouquet of fresh flowers in his lapel, whooping and shouting and cracking his whip as they raced through the narrow streets. The coach was always filled with beautiful women – Jerome's taste for such things was as finely-tuned as his ability to cultivate the finest horses – and that managed to scandalize the wives of his peers. But his obvious joy prompted others, including the influential August Belmont, to master the art of handling teams of horses, and before long the city's streets were filled with Sunday drivers making their presence felt among the lower classes, sometimes by knocking them down.

There were plenty of them. By the last decade of the nineteenth century, New York's population had grown to three-and-a-half million, making it the

Below: For some in the '80s and '90s the parties never started.

Above: *The Mexican War had given Americans a taste of fighting on foreign soil and when, in 1898, newspapers began calling them to battle in Cuba they were quite ready.*

Above: *Teddy Roosevelt and his Rough Riders glamorized the idea of fighting foreign wars with their dramatic charge up Havana's San Juan Hill.*

second largest city in the world after London, and three-quarters of all New Yorkers were living below what we politely call the poverty level today. The majority of them worked six eighteen-hour days a week, and still were forced to take in boarders to make ends meet. A third of all Americans lived in cities by then, a dramatic departure from the country's rural tradition, and for the first time the word "ethnic" was becoming part of the American vocabulary. Throughout all of its history, the country had been populated almost exclusively by Northern Europeans, but in the 1880s, when a half-million immigrants arrived, nearly twenty percent of them came from places like Italy and Poland, Greece and Russia. The percentage of arrivals from Southern and Eastern Europe grew to the low seventies by the turn of the century, and the basic image of the average American as a blonde, blue-eyed Protestant that had been the accepted norm for more than three hundred years underwent an abrupt face-lift. In the first twenty years of the twentieth century, close to nine million more of the so-called "new immigrants," a number equal to nearly a quarter of the entire population at the end of the Civil War, made the change undeniable.

The growing pains on both sides of the scale were tough, but the cheap labor was good for the industrialists, and the determination of the newcomers put a new spin on the American Dream. But the goal of Manifest Destiny, the settling of the West, had already been reached, and there was a growing opinion that the country's only salvation was to expand beyond the confining borders dictated by geography. The nativists, who felt the need to prove the superiority of America, and the newcomers, eager to show that they could be as American as anyone, finally found a common ground in super patriotism. Ordinarily it takes a war or the threat of one to stir such feelings, and in 1898 one was thoughtfully provided.

Three years earlier the Cuban people revolted against their Spanish masters, and when thousands of them were slaughtered, Congress passed a resolution recognizing the revolutionary government. President Grover Cleveland refused to sign it or to help the rebels, and the jingoists were appalled. Newspapers, especially those run by Joseph Pulitzer and William Randolph Hearst, took up the cause and began publishing lurid stories of atrocities, real and imagined. Still Cleveland was unmoved, and he felt exonerated when rioting broke out in Havana after the Spanish offered the Cubans their

Above: *The Spanish-American War took American ships to the Philippines, where Admiral George Dewey sank the Spanish fleet in Manila Bay.*

independence. The riots prompted him to dispatch the battleship *Maine* to protect evacuating Americans, and she had no sooner steamed into Havana's harbor than she was mysteriously blown up. To this day, no one knows whether the explosion was accidental or deliberate, but the newspapers chose to call it treachery, and although Spain had agreed to all the American demands to free Cuba, nothing could satisfy the public mood but to go to war.

It began, oddly enough, in the Philippines, where Admiral George Dewey smashed the Spanish fleet in Manila Bay, followed quickly by American annexation of Hawaii on the grounds that the islands were strategically necessary to maintain American naval superiority in the Pacific. It wasn't long before the fighting reached Cuba itself, and three months after it began, the Spanish-American War was over. At a cost of four hundred lives to bullets and five thousand to tropical diseases, the American sphere of influence was increased by Puerto Rico in the Caribbean and Guam in the Pacific, not to mention the Philippines. The war also gave the country a new breed of cheerleader, the hero of the battle of San Juan Hill, Colonel Theodore Roosevelt.

Left: *The glamor of the three-month war was firmly in the hands of Colonel Theodore Roosevelt.*

These pages: *A free gold watch just for buying a magazine, a chance to pick up gold nuggets as big as your fist from the streams of the Yukon ... who could wish for a better time to be alive and to be an American than the 1890s?*

City streets were filled with the less fortunate, to be sure, but the living rooms of turn-of-the-century America offered plenty of distractions, from an Erector set for the kids to a stereopticon for Grandma, and books for all.

These pages: *Henry Ford rode into the new century in a contraption that would change everything. The telephone, meanwhile, had already changed thousands of American lives.*

BIGGER AND BETTER

At the beginning of the year 1900, Americans were sharply divided over whether the new century began on January first or twelve months later, but they agreed enthusiastically that their country's moment had arrived. Business had never been better, farmers boasted that their barns were bulging, prices were low and wages up, and on Wall Street it was said that if a man couldn't make a fortune it was his own fault.

It was a good time to stop and look back at what American ingenuity had created. Electric lights, telephones and talking machines were making life easier, and after just two short years since automobiles were introduced some eight thousand families owned one. If you had the means, and an unprecedented number of Americans did, you could go abroad on a luxurious steamship or you could take a train to

any one of six National Parks, including the recently-opened Mount Ranier.

The country had dipped its toe in international waters, and if the Filipinos and the Cubans were resisting Americanization, it was assumed they'd soon see the error of their ways and that if they didn't the Marines would persuade them. Meanwhile, the European powers were flexing their muscles in China, and America considered it part of her destiny to get a piece of the action and save the Chinese from themselves. The Chinese didn't see it quite that way, but the combined forces of the Europeans managed to put down their rebellion with the considerable help of the Americans, fighting for the first time as part of a multinational force on foreign soil. The Americans also won the Olympics in Paris that year.

The euphoria hit a snag in 1901, when the

hugely popular President William McKinley was assassinated and replaced by Theodore Roosevelt. It was hard not to like the new President, but just as hard to understand him. A Harvard man from New York, he represented the leisured class, but the word leisure didn't seem to be in his vocabulary. At forty-two he was younger than any of his predecessors and he had the energy of a man half his age. He had been a rancher in the Dakotas, a big game hunter and an impulsive leader in the recent war. He had rooted out corruption as Governor of New York and clipped the wings of some the toughest political bosses in the country. It was not for nothing that the men who ran Washington held their breath when Teddy moved his children and his menagerie of hunting trophies into the White House. "I shall go slow," he reassured them. But it was a promise he couldn't keep.

Four months later, he seemed to have taken leave of his senses when he ordered a lawsuit against J.P. Morgan for violation of a law forbidding restraint of trade in the formation of a corporation to bring all the railroads together under his wing. Morgan was shocked speechless. He and men like him had been consolidating companies for years, and if there was a law against it, well, there was a law against jaywalking, too. And to add insult to injury, this young upstart of a President had neglected to warn him in advance. It was a shabby thing to do, whined Morgan. After all, hadn't he single-handedly headed off a depression back in 1895 by loaning money to the government? Sure, he made seven million dollars

on the deal, but he had saved the country and he expected to be left alone to run his own business in his own way. The case went to the Supreme Court, Morgan lost and his railroad trust was dissolved. J.P. Morgan was hardly left destitute, but the suit gave Wall Street a case of the jitters, and the average wage-earner began to wonder if the day might be at hand when he wouldn't owe his soul to the Company Store any longer. The President himself was smiling broadly, as only he could smile, and he told reporters he had learned a good rule of life on an African safari when a wise old chief told him to "speak softly and carry a big stick."

Above left: *The assassination of President McKinley in 1901 placed Theodore Roosevelt in the White House.*

Above: *When Thomas A. Edison developed electric lamps in 1879, he had already invented the phonograph.*

He took his stick to Pennsylvania next. Coal miners had gone on strike. The economy was in danger of grinding to a halt, the strikers themselves were suffering and the owners were determined not to talk to them. They made no bones about the fact that they despised John Mitchell, who had organized the walkout; one of them even ordered him banned from the mines because he might endanger the morals of the children who were working there. Roosevelt called them all together to meet Mitchell in the White House, with himself representing the third party in the dispute, the public. Nothing like that had ever been done before, but it turned out to be nothing more than a shouting match and the strike went on. When the President ordered federal troops to get ready to start digging coal, J.P. Morgan, of all people, brought the owners together and formed a commission to reopen the mines. Eventually the unions got what they wanted, too, and the people had a new hero. It was a revolutionary idea that the men with the gold didn't necessarily rule and that the man in the White House was the President of all the people. They responded by voting against big city and state political machines; reformers started attacking the problems of the poor, and writers began turning over rocks exposing the wicked ways of men like John D. Rockefeller, who himself developed a social conscience the like of which the world had never seen. Happy days were here again and most Americans were walking on clouds. They didn't know it, but soon they'd be able to soar over them.

On August 1, 1903, M.C. Krarup and E.T. Fetch drove their Packard touring car into New York after a fifty-two-day trip from San Francisco. The country was electrified by the idea, but four months later, when another pair of daredevils, Wilbur and Orville Wright, flew a motorized flying machine across the beach at Kitty Hawk, North Carolina, nobody noticed. Orville went first. He was airborne for twelve seconds and flew one-hundred-and-twenty feet. About an hour later, Wilbur covered one-hundred-and-seventy-five feet; then Orville made two-hundred feet. They knew that their three years of experimenting had paid off when Wilbur soared eight-hundred-and-fifty-two feet in fifty-nine seconds. But when

Right: *The first telephone exchange was installed at New Haven, Connecticut, in 1878, thanks to Alexander Graham Bell.*

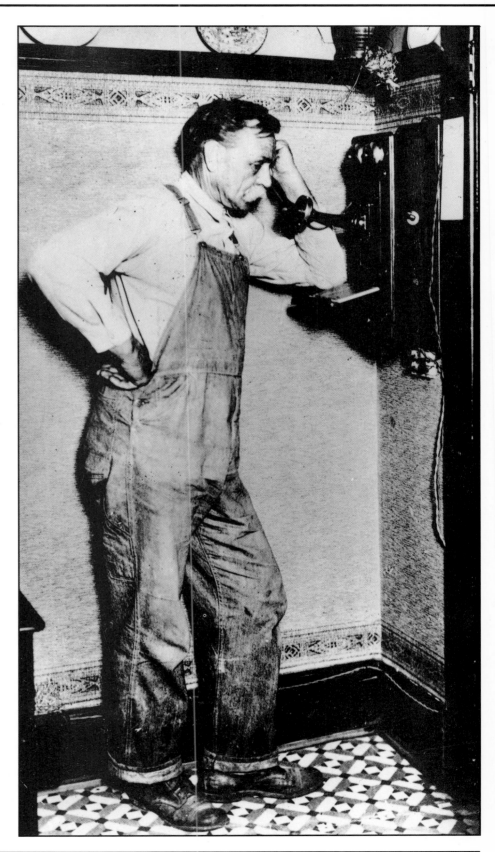

they wired their father back in Dayton, Ohio, to "Inform Press," even their hometown paper spiked the story as "impossible." A newspaper in Norfolk, not far from the historic beach, reported the achievement the next day, but when the writer tried to sell the story to other journals, editors turned him down. Even official Washington turned a deaf ear when the Wright Brothers tried to interest the War Department in their invention. It wasn't until four years later that the military brass agreed to have a look, and even then it was only because the British had sent an army man to Dayton to see what the Wrights were up to. The invitation didn't come a moment too soon. In a few months, Wilbur would set a new record by flying seventy-five miles.

But even in 1907 the War Department had little time for flying machines. President Roosevelt had just announced that the United States fleet was going to take a Pacific cruise. He was interested in impressing the Japanese, who were beginning to flex their muscles, but he was just as interested in a good show, and the sixteen battleships, all appropriately painted white, were about as showy as anything he had at his command. The whole affair gave congressmen and military experts bad bouts of indigestion. Not only would the Atlantic Coast be left vulnerable to attack, but it was a good bet that the Emperor of Japan was already revving up the engines of his torpedo boats. But the President brushed it all aside and the Great White Fleet headed down the coast of South America, through the Straits of Magellan and back up the other side. They were given a hero's welcome wherever they went, and when they hit the California Coast, cities and towns fought with one another for the honor of receiving them. They made it to San Francisco in time for the Fourth of July celebration and three days later turned west. Roosevelt had already announced that they'd come back though the new Suez Canal, making it an around-the-world journey, but even he wasn't sure they'd get beyond Japan. They did, as it turned out. Even the Japanese seemed happy to see them. The ships arrived home less than two weeks before the self-imposed end of Roosevelt's presidency, and

Above: *Bicycle builder Orville Wright managed to stay aloft in a machine he called an airplane for twelve seconds above the beach at Kitty Hawk, North Carolina, on December 17, 1903 while his brother and fellow inventor, Wilbur, watched in wonder.*

Left: *When war came in 1918, and young men marched away to fight the forces of the German Kaiser, the women they left behind supported them by showing up for work in the factories that produced the weapons the soldiers they called "Doughboys" needed to bring a quick end to the so-called "war to end all wars."*

they put a huge exclamation point at the end of an incredible era. As the former President headed off for an African safari, J.P. Morgan drank a toast to the health of the lions.

T.R. rode off into the sunset confident that he had left America a better place than he had found it. He would eventually try making a comeback to correct the wrongs of his hand-picked successor, William Howard Taft, but most Americans felt they were much better off than they ever had been. Except for the women. They had been clamoring for the right to vote since the Civil War, but it was still an uphill battle. They were making an impact on other fronts, though. A woman named Carry Nation was making headlines smashing up saloons with a hatchet; Ida Tarbell, intent on smashing Standard Oil, had earned the name "muckraker" from the President himself;

Emma Goldman was winning converts to the idea that anarchy was the best solution to everybody's problem, and Mother Jones was intent on improving the lives of working class families. There were thousands of others like them, but though many thoughtful men agreed that feminism had its place, it most assuredly wasn't in a voting booth. And many women agreed. The right to vote had a corollary: the next thing, they said, would be female public officials, a filthy business as far as most women were concerned. As one of them pointed out, "men have no right to lay the burden upon us."

But the cause had caught fire in England, and when news of violent protests there reached America, the greatest burden of all seemed to be the lack of a voice in national affairs. Several influential women, including Mrs. O.H.P. Belmont, the grande dame of

Facing page, top: *Women had some rights in 1912, but without the right to vote they felt they had no way to change their destiny.*

Below: *In 1918, their sons and husbands would be sent to France to help change the world, but women had to wait two more years for the right to vote.*

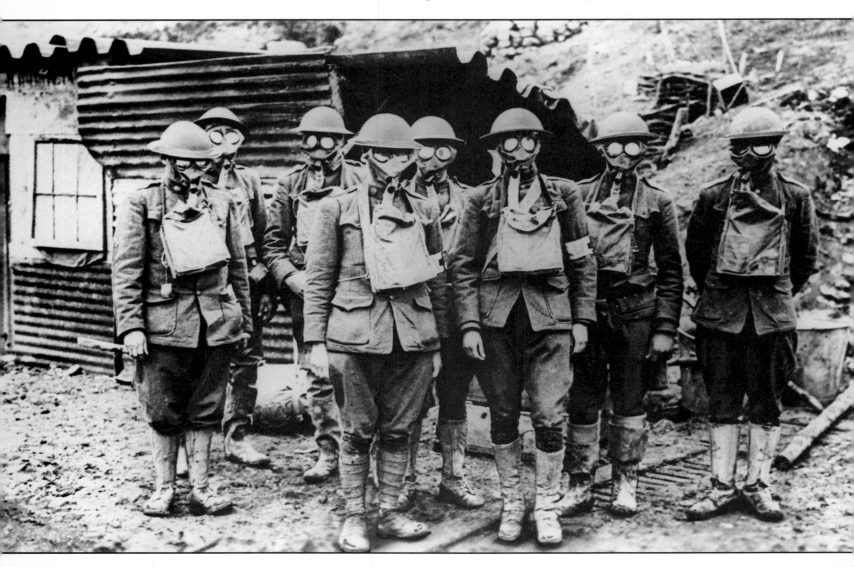

New York society, formed organizations to take up the cause in the mold of their English cousins. In addition to their new enthusiasm they also had money, and a certain amount of glamour which attracted more of the same, and when they organized their first parade in New York in 1910 they expected the earth to move. It didn't. They tried again a year later and this time a hundred men joined the march. Unfortunately for one of them, he was forced to carry a banner that said: "If men can vote, why can't we?" But except for the guffaws, the ladies were ignored once again.

The 1912 march was completely different. It was led by a contingent of fifty women on horseback, very few of whom rode sidesaddle. Their ranks included Inez Milholland, reputed to be the most beautiful woman in America, who had recently stunned the Republican National Convention into silence when she appeared on the floor. Harriet Stanton Blach, the daughter of suffrage pioneer Elizabeth Cady Stanton and the organizer of all three parades, followed close behind, followed in turn by contingents of government typists, waitresses, schoolteachers, actresses, sweat shop workers and society women. The crowds, which had been hostile, melted as the waves of women marched up Fifth Avenue, and they actually cheered when the men's unit, this time more than six-hundred strong, passed by. Though most of the women carried banners, the men chose instead to carry yellow daisies. The procession became a torchlight parade after the sun went down, and it ended with a rally in Carnegie Hall. The next day, *The New York Times* dithered that it was probably inevitable that women would have the vote "and play havoc with it for themselves and society." But it was a voice in the wilderness. The parade had proven that it was a cause as important to shop girls as to women like Mrs. Belmont. Fifteen thousand of them had marched, another fifty thousand had cheered them on. It took a while longer, but finally, on August 26, 1920, enough states had ratified the Constitution's Nineteenth Amendment in time for women to help make Warren G. Harding President of the United States.

Left: *Elizabeth Cady Stanton (right) shocked even fellow feminists like Susan B. Anthony (left) by suggesting that women should have the vote.*

These pages: *They called themselves "Suffragettes," but women like Carrie Chapman Catt (left) and Susan B. Anthony (above), and others who carried banners and made speeches, fought for many more rights for women than the power of the vote. The Amendment to the Constitution that gave American women the right to vote was ratified on August 26, 1920.*

THE ROARING TWENTIES

These pages: *The Constitution's 18th Amendment made it illegal to make, sell or import any intoxicating liquor.*

In Chicago, officials dumped beer into Lake Michigan, and in New York they even poured gallons of whiskey into the sewers.

The First World War established the United States as a giant on the world stage. Though Americans went into it kicking and screaming, after managing to stay neutral until it was nearly over over there, once they were committed, every citizen rallied around the flag and more than four million of their sons went off to lick the German Kaiser, mostly on the battlefields of France. But in addition to putting teeth into the idea that democracy could spread to the rest of the world, even if it took a little force, the war had fascinating side effects on the American democracy. It provided the impetus for female suffrage, championed as vital to the unity of the country, and it tipped the balance against tippling with a Constitutional amendment making it illegal to sell or drink alcoholic beverages.

It was hardly a new idea. The temperance movement began picking up steam after the Civil War, when women who had been active in the Abolitionist cause took on demon rum as the arch-villain in the destruction of the American family. Over the years the reformers managed to get alcohol banned in all but seventeen of the forty-eight states, and most employers had served notice on their workers that they'd be fired if they took as much as a single drink, not just on the job, but even in the privacy of their own homes. Meanwhile, the temperance movement marched onward and upward toward that glorious day when padlocks snapped shut on the doors of saloons in every part of the country.

But, as it turned out, Congress wasn't very successful in legislating temperance. In fact, many people who never had a drinking problem before developed one. They were convinced that their personal liberty was being compromised, and they believed that the only way to eliminate the onerous law was to break it. Most interesting of all, publicans who had traditionally made their barrooms off-limits to women were perfectly willing to let them through the doors of their clandestine watering holes, and for the first time in the history of the republic women were drinking outside their own homes.

One of the problems was enforcement. It had never dawned on the lawmakers that Prohibition wouldn't be as popular as a tax cut and they didn't hire many special agents to keep an eye on things. Most of the G-men were zealous, but they relied on local police for much of their legwork and the latter were easily bribed. On the other side of the coin were the bootleggers, who brewed their own booze or

Below: When he was a young man in Ohio, folks always told Warren Gamaliel Harding he'd make a "dandy-looking president." He did. Mr. Harding became the 29th president in 1921.

Above: The temperance movement grew from women's crusades dating back to the Civil War.

smuggled it down from Canada and up from the Caribbean. The market was incredibly thirsty and the potential profits were fabulous – government accountants estimated the take to be some eighteen billion dollars a year. It was only natural that the new businessmen would go to any lengths to eliminate competition.

There wasn't a city in the country that didn't have its hierarchy of gangsters with fast cars and machine guns, jealously guarding their territories, but the most memorable example of the mayhem Prohibition produced was on the streets of Chicago. The territories were fairly well-defined there even before the new law went into effect. A florist named Dion O'Banion controlled all the vice in the inner city and the suburbs belonged to Johnny Torrio. But the Eighteenth Amendment created a whole new ballgame, and even before it was ratified Torrio began buying breweries. With the market cornered, he was able to set prices as high as fifty dollars a barrel, but his trucks still weren't welcome on the same streets with O'Banion's flower deliverers. Then one day, as O'Banion was arranging a funeral bouquet in his shop, three unidentified customers marched

Above: *When Al Capone's gang of Chicago gangsters mowed down seven members of a rival gang on Valentine's Day, 1929, no jury would convict Scarface Al. He finally went to jail on tax-evasion charges.*

Left: *The twenties ended with a $26 billion bang on Wall Street on October 29, 1929.*

Above: *In New York's Chinatown, gangs went to war to control opium and gambling dens.*

in and shot him dead. Among the floral tributes at his funeral was a huge basket of roses signed, simply, "from Al." It was from Torrio's bodyguard, a recent arrival from New York named Alphonse Capone. It was unthinkable that Al had fired the fatal shots; everyone was convinced that Torrio was the perpetrator, and in a few weeks Johnny went to his reward in a hail of bullets, leaving Al in charge. It wasn't quite a foregone conclusion, though, and Capone found himself engaged in a gang war that lasted four years. A lot of hoodlums died violently, but none of the bullets hit any innocent bystanders until February 14, 1929, when seven gangsters, one of whom turned out to be a casual visitor, were cut down in a Clark Street garage by men dressed as police officers. The Valentine's Day Massacre made Capone the undisputed boss of Chicago, and although no one could pin the crime on him, it also made him the country's most famous mob boss. It took the authorities a few more years to catch up with him, and when they finally nailed him for income tax evasion Al said it was a clear case of discrimination.

But not every American went through the 1920s in an alcoholic haze dodging machine gun bullets. There were plenty of other things to think about. War-weary voters had bought Warren G. Harding's pledge of a return to "Normalcy," and made him their President. But Mr. Harding turned out to be just another pretty face with not much, apparently, going on behind it. "Normalcy," it developed, was a throwback to the Grant administration, and while the President smiled charmingly, the boys in the back room worked tirelessly to give big business a free hand to get bigger. Some of them also managed to get richer themselves, and even cabinet members got involved in the illegal leasing of oil reserves in Teapot Dome, Wyoming, and Elk Hills, California. The oil had been stockpiled for the Navy to use in the event of an emergency, and although the idea of "national security" hadn't come into vogue yet, the public was shocked to learn that both the Secretary of the Navy and the Secretary of the Interior had accepted bribes from oilmen. And to add insult to injury, at the end of the trial, which lasted through most of the decade, the men who paid the bribes were acquitted, reinforcing the idea that the rich were above the law.

Meanwhile, all America was determined to get rich. A boom hit Wall Street in 1922 and even shoeshine boys were getting in on the action. A small down payment was all that was required, rising stock values would take care of the rest, and then some, and it wasn't uncommon for formerly-poor

Above: *Declaring that anyone who lived only for work was a sucker, young people of the 1920s had to find some way to pass the time. Women, who called themselves "flappers," bobbed their hair, hiked their skirts and learned a dance called the shimmy. And if some people were shocked, well, as they said in those days, "What the hey!" That was the point.*

families to move out of the old neighborhood in a flashy car. All it took was a hot tip, and there were plenty of those. The idea of getting something for nothing took the country by storm and there was no shortage of sharp salesmen to promote it. The traditional-minded who were uneasy about speculating in stocks and bonds were gulled into buying land in Florida and Southern California on the theory that real estate was a sure thing. Most of them would have been better off if they had invested their money in Irish Sweepstakes tickets.

But even the losers felt like winners in the Roaring Twenties. Henry Ford had used automation to make a car in every garage an attainable goal. People could escape from their humdrum lives in an ornate movie palace, and they knew every lurid detail about the lives of the glamorous people whose images were flickering on the screen. Film stars were the new royalty and all it seemed to take to join their ranks was good looks and a little luck. Nearly everyone had a radio by then and advertising was helping them find ways to make their bodies smell better, to make their teeth whiter, to get rid of unsightly dandruff and to cultivate a little sophistication with

a cigarette as a prop. Advertising became such an important part of the American lifestyle that Bruce Barton, one of the industry's pioneers, noted with a perfectly straight face that if Jesus Christ had been about His Father's business in the 1920s, He would surely have been an advertising man.

Others were relieved that the Second Coming didn't occur in the Jazz Age. It might have spoiled the fun. Sigmund Freud's work had recently been translated into English, and the newly sophisticated decided that the sexual repression handed down from the Puritans was precisely what was wrong with the country. Almost as though they considered it their patriotic duty, women began wearing form-fitting clothes with hemlines shockingly hiked above the knee. They cut their hair short, rolled their stockings down and danced wildly to jazz music calculated to shock their parents. They appeared on beaches and lakeshores in revealing, one-piece bathing suits and openly read "confession" magazines right out there in public.

It wasn't as though they didn't have a serious thought in their heads. Most states passed laws requiring youngsters to stay in school until they

THE NEW COMMANDER CONVERTIBLE CABRIOLET FOR FOUR

An open roadster or a closed car as you wish. Windows can be raised with top down. Comfortable rumble seat in rear deck.

were at least sixteen and more young people than ever were going on to college. Europeans snickered at the idea that they were earning degrees in such things as animal husbandry and accounting, but the new theory of progressive education was that schools should be turning out useful members of a productive society and not cultured elitists. If the Europeans didn't approve, America had folded in on itself anyway, and nobody much cared what they thought. Congress had even closed the Golden Door, in fact, by establishing immigration quotas based on population percentages existing before 1890, before all those Mediterraneans began arriving. It was all part of a blossoming of bigotry that saw, among other things, the rebirth of the Ku Klux Klan, whose anti-Catholic, anti-Jewish, anti-black and anti-Communist rantings attracted more than five million members by the middle of the decade, at the same time as Fascism was on the rise in Italy and Nazism in Germany. Fortunately, the blossom withered in America and faded into history, along with flappers, bathtub gin and all the other fads, from six-day bicycle races to dance marathons, flag pole-sitting and Mah-Jongg. The Roaring Twenties ended not

with a bang, but with a whimper.

The hangover was the Great Depression, which began on October 29, 1929, when more than sixteen-million shares of stock were traded in a single afternoon. The bubble had been pushed to bursting point by an average increase in the price of stocks by more than three hundred percent in less than five years, and the crash was probably inevitable even though President Herbert Hoover reassured the public that lower prices would lure new money into the market, and that prosperity was sure to continue. But it didn't. The factories were still producing goods, but the warehouses were full, and workers on the assembly lines weren't earning enough to buy the things they made. Besides, most of them were in debt. Almost every major purchase the average American made in the twenties was on the installment plan and good times, along with good advertising, had produced a buying binge.

The stock market lost some forty billion dollars before the end of the year, and wages were cut in half for those lucky enough still to have jobs. Women who had gone to work during the war found themselves housewives again and the servants they

Above: *The Studebaker Commander, a dream machine if ever there was one. With a convertible top and four seats, there was no better way to command attention. There were nine million cars on America's roads in 1920. Ten years later, there were 26.5 million, an average of about one car for every five American citizens.*

Left: *After November 20, 1920, when Pittsburgh's radio station KDKA, the world's first, went on the air.*

Above: *For thousands of families there was no way to pluck the "free entertainment" from the air.*

Above: *The Charleston, introduced in 1925, was the first of the new dances anyone could master and everyone did.*

had hired fell by the wayside. Young people who had been on their own went back home, too, and those who had been planning to get married put their plans on hold. When the marriage rate dropped, so did the birthrate. College enrollments dried up, too, and hundreds of thousands of people were wandering around the country looking for jobs that weren't there. There were a few bright spots, but not many. Radio soap operas helped most families to take their minds off their own troubles at home, and although drinking was still illegal, the speakeasies and nightclubs thrived, as did vaudeville houses and movie theaters. Not many new cars were sold, but people kept the old ones running and gasoline sales actually went up. So did cigarette consumption, as Americans muddled through, wondering how it could be possible that a country bursting with natural resources, with the world's largest pool of willing workers and the most sophisticated industrial plant, could have produced so much misery. There was no shortage of villains, from businessmen to government officials, but there were only scattered organized protests. For the most part, Americans decided there was no sense crying over spilled milk and they kept smiling, confident that there was a solution out there somewhere.

They found their white knight in the person of Franklin D. Roosevelt, the wealthy Governor of New York, who told them that the "forgotten man" was his first concern and that frugality, though necessary, shouldn't come at the expense of starving people. Millions were hungry, but few were near the starvation level, and businessmen condemned the candidate as a "traitor to his class," but in 1932 the voters responded to his optimism and made him their President.

Facing page: The explosion of the zeppelin Hindenburg *in Lakehurst, N.J., on May 6, 1937, killed thirty-six and ended hope for the future of lighter-than-air transport.*

Left: *President Franklin Delano Roosevelt led America out of the Depression by proposing massive public works projects he called his "New Deal."*

THE WORLD OF TOMORROW

In the year 6939, if all goes according to plan, our descendants will be reading *Gone With The Wind*, singing *Flat Foot Floogie* and tapping their feet to *Stars and Stripes Forever*. Among other things, they'll meet Mickey Mouse and study a Sears Roebuck catalogue, not to mention *True Confessions* magazine. Thanks to a time capsule buried on the site of the 1939 New York World's Fair, they'll find out how far America had come in the one-hundred-and-fifty years since George Washington's inauguration. The country was still struggling its way out of the Depression, and though a war breaking out in Europe made tomorrow a little uncertain, there was optimism in the air.

But even the most cock-eyed optimists were reaching for their aspirin bottles by March 4, 1933, when Franklin D. Roosevelt was inaugurated. In the previous few months, foreign investors removed their funds from American enterprises and wealthy Americans followed their example. There was hardly a ship bound for Europe whose hold wasn't filled with gold bars, and not enough was left for the banks to stay in business. The crisis was averted by Inauguration Day itself, which was a bank holiday, and because it also happened to be a Friday, Roosevelt had until Monday morning to keep the banking system from collapsing. In the meantime, businesses began refusing to accept checks and even cash. On Monday, the President ordered the banks to stay closed for another four days, during which time the Treasury Department and Reconstruction Finance Corporation provided them with funds. At the same

183

Right: *Around-the-world flier Amelia Earhart (they called her an aviatrix back then) mysteriously vanished with her airplane in 1937 and no trace of her has ever been found.*

Facing page: *The explosion of the zeppelin* Hindenburg *in Lakehurst, N.J., on May 6, 1937, killed thirty-six and ended hope for the future of lighter-than-air transport.*

Left: *President Franklin Delano Roosevelt led America out of the Depression by proposing massive public works projects he called his "New Deal."*

THE
WORLD OF
TOMORROW

In the year 6939, if all goes according to plan, our descendants will be reading *Gone With The Wind*, singing *Flat Foot Floogie* and tapping their feet to *Stars and Stripes Forever*. Among other things, they'll meet Mickey Mouse and study a Sears Roebuck catalogue, not to mention *True Confessions* magazine. Thanks to a time capsule buried on the site of the 1939 New York World's Fair, they'll find out how far America had come in the one-hundred-and-fifty years since George Washington's inauguration. The country was still struggling its way out of the Depression, and though a war breaking out in Europe made tomorrow a little uncertain, there was optimism in the air.

But even the most cock-eyed optimists were reaching for their aspirin bottles by March 4, 1933, when Franklin D. Roosevelt was inaugurated. In the previous few months, foreign investors removed their funds from American enterprises and wealthy Americans followed their example. There was hardly a ship bound for Europe whose hold wasn't filled with gold bars, and not enough was left for the banks to stay in business. The crisis was averted by Inauguration Day itself, which was a bank holiday, and because it also happened to be a Friday, Roosevelt had until Monday morning to keep the banking system from collapsing. In the meantime, businesses began refusing to accept checks and even cash. On Monday, the President ordered the banks to stay closed for another four days, during which time the Treasury Department and Reconstruction Finance Corporation provided them with funds. At the same

time he scrapped the gold standard and provided federal insurance on small bank deposits, prompting thousands to transfer their savings from under the mattress and into the banks. In the next hundred days, Roosevelt worked to stave off problems in other areas with a series of programs he called his "New Deal." The first of them was a Civilian Conservation Corps that put three million men to work on reclamation projects for a dollar a day plus room and board. Next came the Federal Emergency Relief Administration, empowered to give three billion dollars to the states for welfare programs and work projects. Other new agencies helped farmers and middle class homeowners pay their mortgages; they gave Social Security protection to wage earners

and, through the Works Progress Administration, provided jobs constructing roads and parks and public buildings as well as creating an outlet for artists and writers producing everything from Post Office murals to local histories. More than two hundred industries were pledged to follow minimum hour and wage standards to create more jobs, and their workers were given the right to organize unions under the National Recovery Administration. The Public Works Administration was authorized to spend four billion dollars on highways and other projects, including the Grand Coulee Dam in the Pacific Northwest, the biggest public works project in the history of the world, with the possible exception of the Great Wall of China, and the other possible

Above: *More than 34,000 projects, including the Grand Coulee Dam on the Columbia River, were built in the 1930s by the Public Works Administration.*

exception of the Tennessee Valley Authority that brought two-and-a-half million people into the twentieth century with low-cost electricity. There were dozens of other programs, some of which, like the NRA, were eventually declared unconstitutional, and though nearly all of them brought howls of protest from one corner or another, one idea everyone agreed was overdue was the repeal – promoted as a means of providing both employment and badly-needed tax revenue – of Prohibition.

And revenue was a real problem. The national debt more than doubled in the 1930s to nearly four-and-a-half billion dollars, and critics said that it was all because F.D.R. had killed the all-American principle of self-reliance and replaced it with a welfare state. They accused him of every fault, from being a crackpot to promoting Communism. The business community said it could have brought happy days back on its own if it didn't have the government on its back, and the working class was wondering why so many people still weren't working. After the spending spree, the army of the unemployed was still six million strong. On the other hand, there had been twelve million out of work in 1933, and if

businessmen hated the President, the public had stopped hating them.

As far as most Americans were concerned, the World of Tomorrow theme of the '39 Fair was an unfortunate choice of words. Not many of them cared about the world beyond their borders. They believed that they had been suckered into World War I, and if another war was on the way they weren't going to let it happen again. Strict neutrality, which had always been the country's basic policy, became as important to Americans as mom and apple pie, and if the rest of the world wanted to destroy themselves that was their problem. When Mussolini attacked Ethiopia in 1935, there was a groundswell in Washington for a Constitutional amendment forbidding Congress to declare war except if America itself were attacked. When Franco set out to destroy the Spanish democracy in 1936, it was regarded as an internal affair of interest only to

These pages: *Peggy Payne was the winner of the seventh annual Mrs. America contest in 1945, but America's real love that year was the new cars. Americans had been driving their old 1930s models since the war began and they were ready for a change. Eager buyers were forced to wait six months or more for their new Ford or Chevvy.*

Right: *Around-the-world flier Amelia Earhart (they called her an aviatrix back then) mysteriously vanished with her airplane in 1937 and no trace of her has ever been found.*

WE CAN...
WE WILL..
WE MUST !
..Franklin D. Roosevelt

BUY U.S. WAR SAVINGS BONDS & STAMPS *NOW*

The PUBLIC ENEMY

JAMES CAGNEY · JEAN HARLOW
EDWARD WOODS · JOAN BLONDELL

A WARNER BROS
and VITAPHONE
Production

Directed by WILLIAM A. WELLMAN

This page: *On the home front in the Second World War years, everyone pitched in by buying War Bonds and Stamps. One fundraiser at New York's Yankee Stadium sold $10 million worth in a single day. Many bought the stamps along with movie tickets when they went to see James Cagney as John Dillinger in the film, Public Enemy.*

Spaniards. When the Japanese invaded China the following year and sank an American gunboat, America accepted their apology and went right on shipping arms to them. When Hitler annexed Austria in 1938, it was noted that the Austrians spoke German anyway and it was just a family affair. But by 1939 it was also noted that the Americans and the English shared a common language and that, along with the French, they needed help. The law was amended to allow the European democracies to buy things they desperately needed, but only if they picked them up in their own ships and paid cash in advance. Public opinion eventually softened, and by 1940 the law was amended to a "lend-lease" concept that allowed unlimited help to countries threatened by aggression. But, in theory at least, America was still neutral and intended to stay that way. The Japanese changed all that with the bombing of Pearl Harbor in Hawaii on December 7, 1941. The following day, America was in the war with both feet, one in the Pacific and the other in Europe.

Before it was over, more than fifteen million men and women served in the armed forces, and their government spent $330 billion on the war effort. Virtually every citizen, from retirees to youngsters, involved themselves in it in one way or another, and by the time it ended it had changed every one of them. There was no question in anyone's mind that America would be a dominant force in human affairs for a long time to come.

These pages: *After following news of the battles their fathers and brothers were fighting on far-off Pacific Islands with strange-sounding names,* *the best news of all came with the headlines announcing the Japanese surrender in Tokyo Bay on September 2, 1945, the day they called V-J Day.*

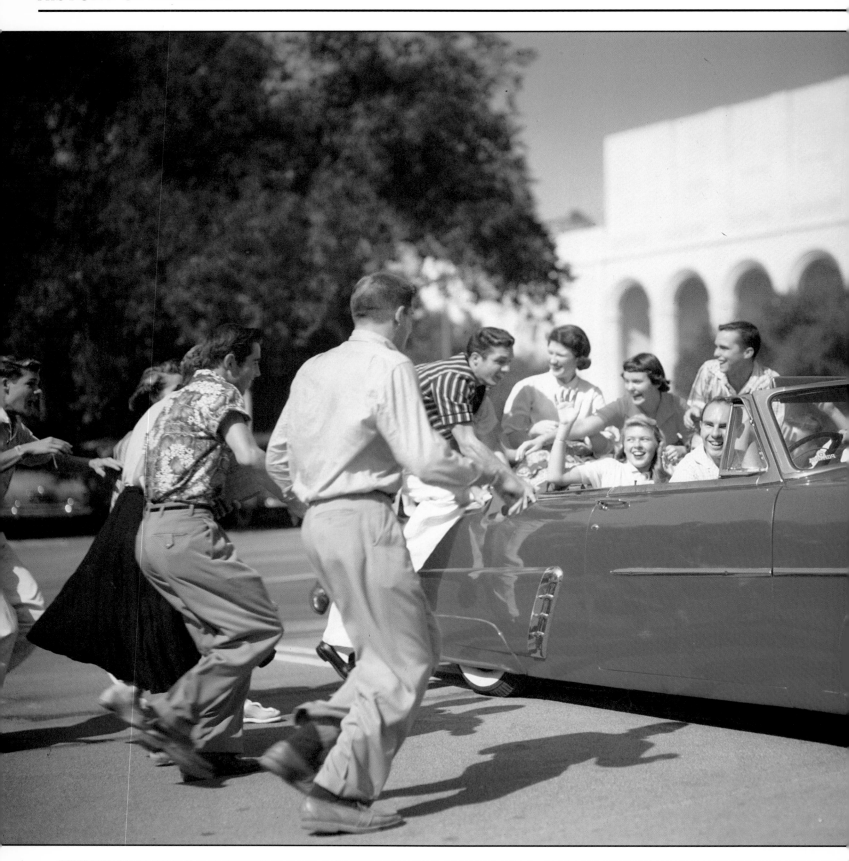

Left: *A new era began when an atomic bomb destroyed the Japanese city of Hiroshima on August 6, 1945.*

Far left: *After the war, "cruising" was a new word for fun. A flashy red convertible was all it took to make lots of new friends.*

THE ATOMIC AGE

The war ended with the biggest bang in history – an Atomic bomb exploded over Hiroshima. The country was sharply divided over whether its mushroom cloud was a sign of the end of civilization or the beginning of a bright new age. But Americans had other things on their minds, too.

During the '30s and the war years, Jews and Catholics found their way into middle-class neighborhoods and blacks had begun working in white collar jobs. Young men who had previously been doomed to lives as wage slaves could get government loans and go into business for themselves, and those who worked for somebody else had stronger unions to look out for their interests. When the war was over, the G.I. Bill of Rights made it possible for any veteran to go to college, a right that had previously been generally reserved for the rich. The G.I. Bill also made it easy for them to buy houses and start families in the suburbs, and hundreds of thousands of them did, changing the face of America from simple rural and urban to something different in between. The biggest problem the American people faced, said one expert, was "… having to learn to live fifty percent better than they have ever lived before."

But under the euphoria was the nagging fear that another war was inevitable and that, thanks to the atomic bomb, it would surely be the end of mankind. And on the surface, a different kind of war had already started. Everyone agreed that wartime wage and price controls had to go, but businessmen liked the idea of a cap on wages, and organized labor was adamantly opposed to rising prices. The United Automobile Workers fired the first shot in the new war by shutting down General Motors a few weeks after the Japanese surrender. Within a few months a half-million coal miners walked off the job and unions announced that they were about to shut down all the railroads, a threat that was averted when President Harry Truman threatened to draft all the strikers into the Army. Meanwhile, prices kept going up, and by the end of 1946 the cost of living was a third higher than it had been when the war started. Living was made even tougher by shortages. It was virtually impossible to find fresh meat at any price, and anyone who wanted a new car, which was just about every family in America, found it was necessary to bribe dealers just to be placed on a waiting list.

And there, lurking in the background, were the Russians. International matters never had been very interesting to Americans, except possibly recent immigrants who still had families in the Old Country,

but in the late 1940s it seemed there was no escaping from the world's problems. And, especially, there was no escaping those Russians. Americans were both shocked and frightened by news reports that they were grabbing up territory, enslaving whole populations and exporting their philosophy right up to America's front door in Latin America. Even when they walked out of U.N. sessions they left behind an empty chair as a reminder that the world hadn't seen the last of them yet. Everyone agreed that a state of war existed between what they preferred to call "East and West," but for the time being at least, it was a cold war.

A great many people believed that the Communist menace was every bit as much a domestic problem as an international one, and while the government was implementing plans to rebuild Europe and keep the Cold War from escalating, investigators were looking for Communists under the rocks of official Washington. They found one in 1948 in the person of

Above: *The specter of Communism was raised in the 1949 trial of Alger Hiss.*

Alger Hiss, an editor of *Time Magazine*, who was accused of being a member of the Communist Party and part of an active espionage ring, and although China fell to the Communists and the Soviets built their own atomic bomb as his trials dragged on, Americans became more solidly convinced that the real enemy was right here at home. It was a conspiracy they said, and little by little, anything they didn't like was said to be part of it. When a Congressman proposed relaxing censorship rules covering the movie industry, he was immediately denounced as a Communist. When a Texas college president made a speech defending intellectual freedom, he was fired for his Communistic tendencies.

The changes of the previous two decades were almost too much to bear. Minorities were slipping into the middle class; working people were thumbing their noses at their bosses; the lower classes seemed to be getting a free ride; the rich didn't feel they were much better off than the folks down at the foot of the hill. As far as the majority of Americans were concerned, it all had to be the result of a conspiracy. By the end of the 1940s its name was Communism, and the root of the evil was the New Deal. Even people who had benefited from the Roosevelt programs were quick to denounce them as the Trojan Horse that started the destruction of the American Dream.

The feeling was pervasive in nearly every segment of society, but among the strongest supporters in the fight against the new so-called un-Americanism were the children of immigrants looking for ways to show that they were as American as the next guy, and Catholics following the lead of Pope Pius XI, who warned the faithful against Atheistic Communism as far back as 1937. The hero of them all was the son of Irish immigrants introduced to the cause by a Catholic priest. Joseph McCarthy of Wisconsin had been a member of the United States Senate for four years, and he was looking for an issue that could get him reelected when he met Father Edmund Walsh of Georgetown University, who had recently written a scathing book denouncing the evils of Communism. McCarthy's constituents were already railing against Eastern intellectualism, which most of them believed was just another name for Communism, and when Father Walsh assured him that the issue would still be very much alive for the next election, the Senator had his cause.

His first salvo was aimed at the State Department, which he said was a glaring hotbed of Leftists, and Secretary of State Dean Acheson, a dangerous "diplomat in striped pants." "I hold here in my hand," he told his audience, "a list of names known to the Secretary of State as members of the Communist Party who nevertheless are still shaping our foreign policy." No one ever saw the list, but over the next several weeks he repeated the charges in other speeches. When a Senate subcommittee investigated and found there was no substance to them, McCarthy announced that Owen Lattimore, an occasional State Department advisor, was "the top Russian espionage agent" in America. Lattimore's name was cleared but McCarthy's became a household word.

The Communists themselves pushed him off the front pages when North Korean forces invaded South Korea in June, 1950. The United Nations retaliation and America's part in it defused charges that Communist-driven foreign policy had abandoned the Orient, and for a time the Truman Administration was exonerated. But as the war dragged on and losses mounted, fighting Communists lost some of its luster, and by November, when the Chinese

Below: *Low-cost Government loans helped World War II veterans buy new homes, and builders responded by creating new suburbs filled with "dream houses" they couldn't resist.*

jumped in, the situation became grim. At home, meanwhile, there was a wave of scandal that included influence-peddling among government officials; basketball stars in a half-dozen colleges were accused of accepting bribes, and at West Point members of the football team were cheating in examinations, while all over the country juvenile delinquency was growing to alarming proportions. And in the midst of it all, a congressional committee was investigating organized crime in front of the largest television audience ever assembled up to that time.

There was very little good news in America by the end of 1951. On top of everything else, President Truman had dismissed General Douglas MacArthur for insubordination, and the people, who perceived the General as the architect of the victory against the Japanese, were shocked. MacArthur had no sooner faded from the headlines when Senator McCarthy came back into the public eye with charges that General George C. Marshall, a hero of the European war and author of the Marshall Plan for the recovery that followed, was involved in a Communist conspiracy "so black as to dwarf any in the history of man." He didn't offer proof, but by then he didn't have to. No less a person than Senator Robert Taft, the Founding Father of modern Republican Conservatism said, "Whether Senator McCarthy has legal evidence, whether he has overstated or understated his case is of lesser importance. The question is whether the Communist influence in the State Department still exists." And soon the question went beyond the State Department.

The 1952 election that swept Dwight D. Eisenhower into the White House also returned McCarthy to the Senate, and with the Republicans in the majority, he was made chairman of the Committee on Government Operations, which gave him control of its Subcommittee on Investigations. He made the most of it. The State Department issued an order forbidding its U.S. Information Service from circulating books, artwork and music by Communists and their "fellow travelers." Librarians all over the country got the message and began removing everything from their shelves that might not be politically correct. Many of them even burned the potentially offensive works, including detective stories by Dashiell Hammett and novels by John

This page: *After the years of depression and war, parents made sure their children had advantages they had missed.*

Their daughters all became debutantes, and a teenager without a telephone of her own felt culturally deprived.

Steinbeck. Even Robin Hood was a suspect. After all, the reasoning went, any man who would steal from the rich to give to the poor must be a Communist. At the same time, the F.B.I. was quietly collecting information on real people who might have un-American tendencies. In less than ten years it had accumulated close to a half-million files on organizations and individuals considered potentially dangerous.

In 1954, McCarthy took on the Army, charging that it had promoted a Medical Corps dentist even though he refused to sign a loyalty oath and then committed the unpardonable sin of refusing to explain himself to McCarthy's Subcommittee. The Secretary of the Army responded with some charges of his own, including one that the Senator and members of his staff had arranged special treatment for Private G. David Schine, a former consultant to their Subcommittee. McCarthy retaliated with an accusation that the Secretary was a Communist sympathizer himself, and was using Private Schine as a pawn to keep the Subcommittee from exposing him. The televised hearings on the matter lasted more than a month, and for his supporters it was McCarthy's finest hour. But in the end it proved to be his worst hour, and when it was over all he could find left to say was "I don't know what I did wrong."

The man who brought McCarthy down was Joseph Welch, a Boston attorney representing the Army. After three weeks of frustration, the Senator broke in on the counselor's questioning to announce that a young man in Welch's firm was a member of an organization that was "the bulwark of the Communist Party." Hardly missing a beat, the avuncular lawyer looked McCarthy in the eye and said, "Until this moment, Senator, I think I never gauged your cruelty or your recklessness." He went on to describe his associate as a brilliant young lawyer with a bright future, except that now, "he shall always bear a scar inflicted by you." After hinting that McCarthy's own chief lawyer was a member of the same legal professional association, Welch ended by saying, "Have you no sense of decency, sir?" The message was not lost on the television audience and McCarthyism died in the face of decency.

Above: *The 1950s began with yet another war. But the action in Korea was called a "conflict," even though it caused 157,000 American casualties and cost the U.S. some $15 billion. It ended with an armistice signed on July 27, 1953.*

Above: *Richard Nixon earned a national reputation with microfilm of secret documents he said was in a hollow pumpkin ready for delivery to Communist agents.*

Right: *Evelyn Ay had her year in the sun when she became Miss America in 1954. The pageant has been held in Atlantic City since 1921, when Margaret Gorman won the crown.*

Far right: *The real King of the 1950s was a country boy from Memphis, Tennessee, named Elvis Presley, who burst on the scene with a recording of a song called "That's All Right."*

YOUTHQUAKE

By the beginning of the 1960s more than half of all Americans were under thirty and, by and large, they represented a privileged class their grandparents never dared dream of entering. Postwar prosperity had touched nearly every family, and the traditional working class had become solidly middle class, with split-level houses, color television sets and electric can openers. Many of them had two cars and, as soon as they were old enough to drive, their children could have one, too. In fact, their children could have just about anything they wanted, and it was a foregone conclusion that they'd go to college when the time came. No generation in the history of the country had as many advantages, and when they began protesting against American values, the older generation was mystified.

The trend began in the '50s with writers like Allen Ginsberg and Jack Kerouac, who were shocked by the excesses of McCarthyism and the rush to unquestioning conformity and wasteful materialism. Their answer was to reject conventional society and remake themselves in their own image. The image

These pages: *The ghost of the '60s still walks. Demonstrators still appear on city streets and the children of former hippies still throng outdoor rock concerts. But thirty years after young people took it on themselves to change the world, today's protesters and the music that inspires them sometimes seem tame by comparison.*

the self-styled beatniks created was the direct opposite of the buttoned-down, grey-flanneled mainstream strivers around them, and when they weren't calling attention to themselves with their unorthodox clothes, they managed to shock the Establishment by advocating free love and drugs and rejecting traditional religion in favor of mysticism. It was largely an underground culture, though, and eventually other young people remade the movement itself into something more pervasive and intense. Their message became one of love and peace, and if some of the threads of violence carried through, middle-class students flocked to the idea of living a simple, independent life as "flower children."

In many ways they were more deeply caught up in conformity than their parents. If their fathers still wore shirts and ties and their mothers owned white gloves, they protested against affluence by wearing blue jeans, thoughtfully made old- and faded-looking by manufacturers who also discovered that they could boost sales by tearing holes in them. But the most striking difference between the younger generation of the '60s and their earlier counterparts, in America at least, was their social consciousness and political activism. They organized under the banner of the New Left, and first made their presence felt by leaving the country in 1959 to cut sugar cane in Cuba alongside the followers of their new heroes, Fidel Castro and Che Guevara. A year later they went into the segregated South under the banner of the Student Non-violent Coordinating Committee, literally to risk their lives organizing the sit-ins and voter registration drives that began the civil rights movement. In 1962 they reorganized Students for a Democratic Society, which took up such causes as help for the poor and civil rights for minorities, but made its strongest impact on college campuses themselves with demands for more "relevance" in the classroom and less authority beyond it.

The New Left made its impact felt on society at large when the widening Vietnam War increased draft quotas and their previously non-violent protests took on an ugly edge. The more militant they became, the more hostility they encountered, and their revolution eventually crumbled, but not before they had managed to change the way America looks at itself.

But they didn't do it alone. On January 20, 1961, John F. Kennedy announced that "the torch has been passed to a new generation of Americans," as he took the oath of office as the first President born in the twentieth century. He echoed the feelings of the new generation and they trusted him, and it was one

of the few things older Americans agreed with them about. Kennedy and his wife, Jacqueline, were like a breath of fresh air to intellectuals who had been forced into hiding in the previous decade. In spite of the country's anti-royalist beginnings, presidential families have always had an aura of royalty about them, but this royal family was somehow closer to the people than all the others had been, and they felt an urge to be more like them, often in spite of themselves. And people who wanted to make a difference felt that it was possible for the first time. It was not for nothing that they compared the White House to Camelot, and even if, as has been charged in the years since, there was more style than substance there, the style made everyone proud to be part of a vital enterprise. More important, they were willing to be involved in it. It was a brief encounter, brought to an end in 1963 by an assassin's bullet, but the torch had, indeed, been passed to a new generation.

These pages: *"Never trust anybody over thirty," they chanted, but there were some exceptions in San Francisco's Haight-Ashbury District, a mecca for young people in the '60s. The older generation also often appeared at anti-war rallies in Washington and elsewhere, but the Vietnam War itself was a young man's business.*

Above: *Richard Nixon was elected president on a promise to end the Vietnam War, but he secretly escalated it by extending the fighting into Laos and Cambodia. The longest war in U.S. History ended in 1973 as Nixon began his second term as president.*

inauguration it was done with such strict secrecy that many commanders in the field didn't even know it was happening. When the press reported the expansion two months later, the White House ordered wiretaps not only on members of the press corps, but on key members of the administration as well. And the fourth estate, which had never been popular among the politicians they were watching, became second-class citizens. Nixon the campaigner had also promised to bring the country together, but the knowledge that the war had expanded, combined with the lack of knowledge of how and why, inflamed the anti-war activists. The President met them head-on by hinting that their violence would be met by force. "We have the power to strike back if need be," he said, "and to prevail." He also revealed that radicals recently convicted for disrupting the 1968 Democratic Convention in Chicago had been brought to heel by secret government wiretaps, and that he believed the law requiring warrants for such surveillance didn't apply in cases involving national security. The electronic age had reached the Land of the Free. As had happened to Johnson before him, Nixon's positive accomplishments were eventually swamped in a sea of negatives. He was in the White House when an American became the first man to go to the moon, and his diplomacy reopened the door to China, but for many Americans his place in history is anchored to a scandal known, simply, as "Watergate." It was his undoing, and he might have been able to escape it had it not been for a little electronic bug.

It all started with what the White House dismissed as a "third-rate burglary attempt" on the head-quarters of the Democratic National Committee in Washington's fashionable Watergate complex. But as the story began to unfold in the press, it became obvious that it was part of a larger scandal that included bribery of government officials and spying on private citizens perceived as the President's enemies. Nixon himself managed to stay above the battle until a year after the break-in, when it was revealed that he had installed an elaborate system to tape record conversations secretly in his own office. The tapes eventually provided enough evidence to convict dozens of high Administration officials and left the President himself facing impeachment on charges of misusing the Central Intelligence Agency, the Justice Department, the Federal Bureau of Investigation and even the Internal Revenue Service to keep his political enemies at bay. Nixon, claiming that his only error had been one of poor judgement, and concluding that an impeachment trial would

But fifty thousand members of that generation died in a war halfway around the world in a green hell called Vietnam. Not many Americans could find it on a map, and even fewer had any idea how it all started, but by 1965 American involvement that began ten years earlier with a few advisors and CIA agents had escalated to one-hundred-thousand American troops, and three years later the number jumped again to more than a half-million. It was a war as divisive as the Civil War itself. Flag-waving patriots asserted that America had never lost a war, and whatever it might take she wasn't going to lose this one; but protesters with picket signs were even more assertive, shouting, "Hell no, we won't go!" Passions on both sides overshadowed almost everything else, including President Lyndon Johnson's revolutionary civil rights and antipoverty programs, which in another era might have given him a permanent lease on the White House.

Richard Nixon picked up the lease in the 1968 election. He had promised to end the war, but he didn't say how, and when he made a move to escalate it by bombing Cambodia a few weeks after his disrupt the government, resigned from office on August 9, 1974. Ironically, his Vice President, Spiro Agnew, had already resigned after it was charged that he had accepted bribes in his former position as Governor of Maryland. The man who became President that day had been appointed to the vice presidency by Nixon himself. Gerald Ford, in fact, had never run in a national election. In a later trial that sent Nixon's Attorney General, his Chief of Staff and others to prison, the former President was named an unindicted co-conspirator. He never appeared as a witness during the trial, but his voice dominated the proceedings through the secret tapes he had made to assure his place in history.

Left: *Miss Americas came and went and women began questioning whether beauty pageants were the right way forward.*

Above: *Young people went right on fighting for their own rights as well as the rights of others around the world. They gathered at concerts more often than at demonstrations, and if they drank Coke and Pepsi to protest hunger, well, it's the thought that counts.*

Left: *One of the legacies of the '60s is the way Americans are entertained. People whose grandparents banned burlesque find Madonna innovative and believe that Roseanne Barr's TV family (above) is typically American.*

Left: *Singing in the rain, Woodstock, 1969. For many, this music festival marked the high point of the youth culture of the decade and came to epitomize the "Swinging Sixties."*

Above: *Folk singer Bob Dylan personified the '60s. His home base at Woodstock, N.Y., gave its name to the generation.*

THE THIRD CENTURY

These pages: *By the time Ronald Reagan became president in 1981, Americans were beginning to be known as the "me" generation. Getting rich no matter what it took was only part of it. They were also on a health kick, and quiet country lanes turned to jogging trails as they ran for their lives.*

When America celebrated its two-hundredth anniversary in 1976, the baby boom generation that had dominated the '60s was beginning to celebrate significant birthdays, too. One by one, they were turning thirty. And they were turning inward. They had set out to change the world a few years earlier, but when they looked around and saw the same old problems still there, they began to concentrate on improving themselves rather than society. Interestingly, they did it the same way they had done everything else – together. They joined therapy groups and health clubs, and formed armies of joggers running together as though the grim reaper was following close behind. They went to weekend seminars to have their consciousness raised and to health farms to nibble beansprouts and sweat off unsightly cellulite. They became nostalgic for the past, but only for the "Golden Oldies" of the recent rock music era that had given way to a disco beat, and for the television programs that had been their babysitters, and not for the halcyon days when they spoke up for change and the adult world listened. They seemed to have lost faith in the future, even though their health kick was calculated to make them live through it, and only the here and now seemed to matter. They lost whatever confidence they might have had in the political system, too. In the 1970s, well over half the eligible voters who didn't show up at the polls were members of the same generation that had been so determined to change the world that they managed to have the voting age lowered to eighteen. And the same young people who had slouched through the '60s with dirty clothes and straggly hair suddenly became obsessed with their appearance. Having a healthy tan, a flat stomach and a full wallet was the common goal, and for many of them they were the only goals. People still in college caught the spirit and worked for MBAs that would make them instant managers when they graduated, and guarantee incomes so high that their Social Security tax would be covered by payroll deductions by the end of January. Back in the '60s a young radical named Jerry Rubin had formed the Youth International Party, whose members called themselves Yippies. "We ain't never gonna grow up," he said. "We're gonna be adolescents forever!" But they did grow up. Rubin himself became a pioneer in the concept of "networking," the idea of cultivating friendships that could improve one's own income, and his own friends worked hard to become part of a new youth culture known as "Yuppies," young urban professionals, who were taking materialism to new heights.

As young Americans were looking inward, the country itself had lost all of its former isolationist tendencies, and in the years since World War II had positioned itself solidly on the world stage. Such a thing had been unthinkable only a half-century earlier, when most Americans shared the opinion that it was best to let the rest of the world stew in its own juice. The war changed all that, and presidents from Eisenhower onward began to regard foreign affairs as their primary concern, quite often at the expense of domestic problems. The world itself had changed, to be sure, from the time when George Washington warned his countrymen against foreign entanglements, but modern American presidents had discovered it was more rewarding to be regarded as a world leader; and it was infinitely better to be welcomed in a foreign capital by brass bands than in an American city by angry demonstrators.

But sometimes there are angry demonstrators in foreign capitals, too. In 1979, President Jimmy Carter scored a personal triumph by negotiating a peace treaty between Egypt and Israel, but a few months later the Middle East came back to haunt him and plunge the country into the despair of frustration. When Carter agreed to allow the recently-exiled Shah of Iran into the United States for medical treatment, a screaming mob of followers of the Ayatolla Khomeini responded by storming the American Embassy in Tehran.

At first they said they were only staging a sit-in and that no one would be hurt, but once inside the compound they tied and blindfolded the Americans inside the Chancery Building. Eleven others who had barricaded themselves inside the Embassy itself managed to escape, and though five were recaptured the rest went into hiding for eleven weeks, until the Canadian Ambassador could spirit them out of the country. But the rest weren't so lucky. After about two weeks Khomeini ordered the release of the female and black hostages, but there were still forty-four prisoners left behind. They stayed there exactly four-hundred-and-forty-four days before Carter was able to negotiate their freedom, and they came home, ironically, on Inauguration Day, a few hours after the end of Carter's presidency. The new President, Ronald Reagan, would share the triumph of their homecoming, but his own presidency would eventually be blackened by events outside his own

Above: *Jimmy Carter was almost completely unknown to Americans outside of Georgia, where he was governor, when he became president in 1977.*

country, and the trouble would begin in Iran.

Through the 1970s and into the '80s, the taking of hostages became a basic tactic of international terrorism, particularly in Lebanon, and the American government seemed powerless to do anything about it. Then, in 1986, a Lebanese magazine reported that the United States had secretly sold weapons to the Iranians. The Administration denied it at first, but when the truth was verified, President Reagan went on national television with a denial that the sale had anything at all to do with the release of hostages. In a way, the statement was true. Though it had been proven that missiles were shipped to the Khomeini government, the sale didn't at the time result in freedom for the Americans languishing in Lebanon.

By the end of the month it was revealed that the

Left: *On November 4, 1979, the U.S. Embassy in Tehran, Iran, was overrun and everyone inside taken hostage. Iran's Ayatolla Khomeini was hailed as a hero by his own people, but to Americans this was the face they loved to hate. The hostages were held for 444 days before President Jimmy Carter was able to get them freed on the last day of his presidency, January 20, 1981.*

Above: *After a 1979 revolt by the Sandinista Liberation Front in Nicaragua, the Reagan Administration gave support to its opponents, the Contras.*

funds from the arms deal had been secretly diverted to the Nicaraguan Contras, which had become one of the Administration's favorite charities. Nicaragua had been taken over in a 1979 civil war by the Sandinista Liberation Front, which was overtly anti-American, if not Communist supported, and the Reagan Administration had taken on the cause of its opponents, who called themselves Contras. But the Contras had much less support from the Nicaraguan people, and Congress, fearing involvement in another Vietnam-like rebellion, prohibited all aid for overthrowing the government there. A year later, when it was revealed that the CIA was still involved

in the Contra effort in spite of the ban, Congress cut off all money for military operations in Nicaragua. If the Iranian payments had been diverted as charged, it was a violation of that law.

In the investigation that followed it was revealed that the Administration had been routinely soliciting funds for the Contras from other countries and from private citizens to get around the law, and that when the Israeli government suggested the sale of weapons to Khomeini as a means of freeing hostages, Lieutenant Colonel Oliver North of the National Security Council went to work. More than a thousand missiles went to Iran in 1986 to be used in its war

Above left: *The Nicaraguan war had its share of innocent victims.*

Above: *Many felt that Lt. Colonel Oliver North, accused of selling missiles to Iran and secretly diverting the profits to the Nicaraguan Contras, was more a victim of the war and its politics than a lawbreaker.*

against Iraq. Three hostages were released during the period, but the Iranians didn't take the credit, and at the same time three others were captured. In the meantime, negotiations for the arms sales were turned over to private citizens and details were kept secret from Congress, the Cabinet and possibly even the President himself. When the affair was first made public, Reagan said that he didn't know "the particulars," but six months later he boasted that it "was my idea." The Congressional investigation into the Iran-Contra affair ended in 1987, but the questions it raised may never be answered. Like so many events in American life, Iran-Contra faded away in the glare of other matters. And although Nicaragua dominated the news all through the 1980s, it's a good bet that most Americans can't remember whether they were for the Contras or against them. It's a sure bet they don't remember that U.S. Marines invaded the Central American country in 1912 to collect on a defaulted loan.

Although a great deal of information slipped past them, 1980s Americans were congratulating themselves on having created an information age.

Satellites whizzing around in space made it possible to transmit television pictures to any spot in the world, and fiber optic cables stretched under both the Atlantic and Pacific Oceans, making it possible to carry forty thousand simultaneous telephone calls into either Europe or Asia. By the end of the decade, Americans were averaging five billion minutes of overseas calls a year, and few of them remembered the time in the not too distant past when an international line had to be reserved hours in advance, and usually created a language barrier of static and other background noises. Fax machines allowed pictures and written information to move with the speed of light, and computers were able to talk with one another like teenagers on a day off from school. The technology that made it all possible came from the native Yankee ingenuity that in other eras had given the world such wonders as alarm clocks, six-shooters, steamboats and factory production lines, but in the 1980s the machines themselves usually came with instruction manuals translated from Japanese. It was virtually impossible to buy a television set made in America, and the names most

These pages: *Children whose parents never mastered a typewriter find computer literacy not only easy but fun. And thanks to the promise of electronic home offices, those children may never have to spend time in the traffic jams that were an unpleasant part of the day's work for their parents.*

frequently encountered in traffic jams included Honda, Toyota and Mitsubishi, appearing on the nameplates of cars that may, in fact, have been made in a factory just beyond the freeway interchange, but were regarded as foreign cars nonetheless. If the Japanese had learned the secrets of mass production, they had also mastered the art of marketing, another product of good old Yankee ingenuity. Businessmen were fair game for seminars, and an endless parade of books that might help them become as successful as their Japanese competitors in implementing ideas their own predecessors had invented. But there were other ways to get rich, and that was still central to the American Dream.

The Puritan work ethic had taken a beating in the '60s, and two decades later it was still unfashionable to think that hard work and clean living was the primary road to success. But the Puritans had also been influenced by another facet of the teachings of John Calvin. Before Calvin began redefining Christianity in the sixteenth century, it had been an article of faith that God loved the poor, but he preached that financial success was the real mark of God's favor. In the streamlined world of the 1980s, the goal was still the same in America, even if the traditional means had been swamped in cynicism.

Easy affluence wasn't a brand-new idea; the Colonial New Englanders themselves had discovered

These pages: *Tokyo's Shinjuku District has become a symbol of the electronic revolution that has completely changed America and the rest of the world. The new technology makes it possible to design a building, write a book, or keep track of family finances, faster and easier than ever before.*

a short cut to riches by speculating in land, and in the '80s, people who sold houses they had bought for twenty-thousand dollars insisted they were worth ten times that much, and they had no trouble finding buyers who agreed. Money still tended to stay at the top, where the wealthiest one percent of the population increased their personal income by seventy-four percent. But the poor didn't feel left out; they went out and bought more lottery tickets.

But it wasn't just superstars who were getting rich. Young people in their twenties were collecting six-figure incomes through investment banking. As recently as a decade earlier, the route to a successful business career was to climb the corporation ladder, but the recession of the '70s, coupled to a Middle East oil embargo and the new competition from Japan, had America's corporations in a tailspin. It was apparent to young people that wealth was something that could be created as well as earned, and the rise of new entrepreneurs, especially in the computer industry, created a need for new venture capital. They also found opportunities in mergers and acquisitions that expanded and contracted, changing the face of corporate America.

Like every other boom, it didn't last forever. The beginning of the end came with a plunging Dow Jones Average in October, 1987, and by the following spring more than three hundred thousand people, accustomed to chauffeur-driven limousines, were riding the subway to the unemployment office. Some of the more flamboyant among them were looking at the world through prison bars. But in the end, the money culture went on thriving. A year after the market slipped, nearly four thousand American companies merged with others, or were swallowed up, and the investment bankers earned $1.2 billion.

Nothing lasts forever in America, but trends have a fascinating way of repeating themselves. The conspicuous wealth of the 1980s wasn't much different from the Gilded Age of the last century, except that the players were younger and their toys more exotic. The activism of the '60s had its parallels in the Abolitionist crusades, and the anti-social mood of the decade squared with the feelings of the Hippies' grandparents, who went to great lengths to shock their own parents in the 1920s. The problem of the homeless in America is an old story to people who lived through the Great Depression. The AIDs epidemic is dwarfed by the scourge of influenza that took twenty million lives, including a half-million in the United States, in 1920. We despair that "foreigners," especially the Japanese, are taking over our companies and institutions, but during the 19th

century those corporations relied on foreign funds. Most of the private money that built the railroad system that opened the West came from German and British investors, and even today British interests control more than seven times the number of U.S. companies owned by the Japanese. Foreign influence is, however, far less than it was a hundred years ago.

After the 1980's bubble burst, and the bills started coming due in an era of unemployment and reduced income, Americans began tugging at their bootstraps again. After rejecting the policies of Ronald Reagan and George Bush, goaded on by the populist hard talk of millionaire H. Ross Perot, the mood of the country began to shift again. The voters elected Bill Clinton to lead them, rather than Perot, but the millionaire's message wasn't lost. In a way, America seemed twice blessed: the people were inclined to agree with Perot that change depended directly on them, and the new president – one of the youngest – represented an opportunity for fresh thinking and youthful enthusiasm. In the last decade of the 20th century, it appeared, America had changed its course again, this time to deal with internal problems. It

These pages: Homelessness, the AIDS crisis and other social problems make many wonder if the American Dream may have turned into a nightmare. But those who know America's history know that the Dream has survived worse crises in the past and these problems, too, will eventually be solved.

had happened before, but it doesn't seem likely that the new emphasis on domestic matters will take America back to the days of 19th-century isolationism, or even to Roosevelt's New Deal. However, the 1990s may well be the most fascinating decade in the history of the United States.

Sociologists are fond of pointing out that history repeats itself every thirty years or so, and in many ways they seem to be right. But watching the six o'clock news on television will never be quite like watching an old movie. America has gone through the thirty year cycle ten times since that day when Christopher Columbus's three little ships put ashore in the Bahamas, and the events of those three hundred years could provide the plots for thousands of movies, no two of them alike.

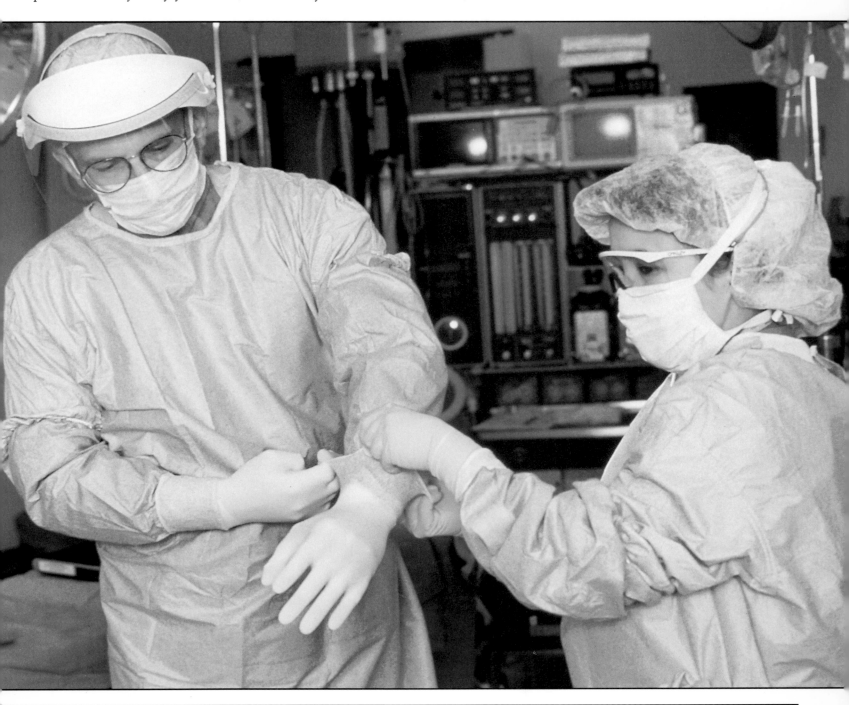

AMERICAN HISTORY TIME LINE

1492	Christopher Columbus discovers the Bahamas.
1497	Sebastian Cabot explores Northeast Atlantic Coast.
1501	Spain imports black slaves to Santo Domingo.
1524	Giovanni da Verrazano sails from the Carolinas to Nova Scotia.
1540	Francisco Vasquez de Coronado explores the Southwest.
1565	St. Augustine, Florida, established.
1579	Sir Francis Drake claims California for England.
1607	Jamestown, Virginia, settled.
1609	Samuel de Champlain establishes Quebec.
1609	Henry Hudson arrives in New York Harbor.
1619	First African slaves imported to Jamestown.
1620	Pilgrims land at Plymouth, Massachusetts.
1624	Dutch settle in New Amsterdam.
1626	Peter Minuit buys Manhattan Island for $24.
1634	Maryland colony established.
1636	Rhode Island founded.
1636	Harvard College established.
1664	British fleet forces New Amsterdam to become New York.
1673	Nathanial Bacon leads revolt against British influence in Virginia.
1682	Robert Cavelier, Sieur de La Salle, claims lower Mississippi for France.
1683	William Penn buys Indian land to create Pennsylvania.
1692	Nineteen persons executed for witchcraft at Salem, Massachusetts.
1699	French settlers establish a colony at New Orleans.
1709	British claim Nova Scotia in Queen Anne's War.
1735	Trial of publisher John Peter Zenger establishes freedom of the press.
1740	Vitus Bering discovers Alaska for the Russians.
1754	French and Indian War begins.
1765	British Stamp Act tax begins rumblings for American Independence.
1770	British troops kill five in Boston Massacre.
1773	Patriots dump British tea into Boston Harbor.
1774	First Continental Congress meets in Philadelphia.
1775	British soldiers and Minutemen skirmish at Concord, Massachusetts.
1776	Declaration of Independence approved.
1777	Stars and Stripes approved as the national banner.
1777	General Washington defeats British at Princeton, New Jersey.
1777	British surrender at Saratoga, New York.

1777 Articles of Confederation adopted.

1779 Naval victory in British waters for John Paul Jones.

1781 British defeat at Yorktown ends the American Revolution.

1782 British recognize American independence.

1787 Northwest Ordinance opens land west of the Alleghenies for settlement.

1789 Constitution, ratified by nine states, declared in effect.

1789 George Washington chosen as first president.

1791 Bill of Rights ratified.

1800 Federal Government moves to Washington.

1801 America's first foreign war fought in Tripoli.

1803 Napoleon sells Louisiana Territory to the U.S.

1804 Lewis and Clark Expedition explores territory from St. Louis to Oregon.

1808 Importation of African slaves outlawed.

1812 Britain and U.S. go to war over seizure of American ships and sailors.

1814 British troops attack Washington D.C. and Baltimore, inspiring writing of the *Star Spangled Banner*.

1815 American victory at the Battle of New Orleans.

1819 Spain cedes Florida to the United States.

1819 American steamship, *Savannah*, makes successful transatlantic voyage.

1823 Monroe Doctrine limits foreign involvement in the Americas.

1825 Erie Canal connects New York with the Great Lakes and the West.

1828 Baltimore and Ohio Railroad, America's first, starts carrying passengers.

1831 Nat Turner leads slave revolt in Virginia.

1836 Texans defeated in the Battle of the Alamo.

1838 Cherokee Indians moved to Oklahoma after gold is found in their Georgia homeland.

1841 First overland wagon train sets out from Independence, Missouri, bound for California.

1842 Oregon Trail established.

1844 Samuel F. B. Morse demonstrates his telegraph.

1846 War with Mexico adds Southwest to U.S. map, including Texas and California.

1846 Americans in California declare an independent republic.

1847 Mormons settle in Utah.

1848 Gold discovered in California.

1848 First Women's Rights Convention held at Seneca Falls, New York.

1853 Commodore M. Perry negotiates trade with Japan.

1859 Petroleum discovered at Titusville, Pennsylvania.

1859 John Brown attempts capture of Federal arsenal at Harpers Ferry, Virginia.

1860 Abraham Lincoln elected president.

1860 Pony Express begins carrying mail between California and Missouri.

1861 Seven southern states secede from the Union and form the Confederate States of America.

1861 Civil War begins at Fort Sumter in Charleston, South Carolina.

1862 Homestead Act grants free land to western settlers.

1863 President Lincoln signs Emancipation Proclamation.

1865 Robert E. Lee surrenders to Ulysses S. Grant at Appomattox Court House, Virginia.

1865 President Lincoln assassinated.

1865 Slavery abolished by Constitutional Amendment.

1866 Ku Klux Klan secretly formed.

1867 U.S. buys Alaska from the Russian Tsar.

1868 President Andrew Johnson acquitted in impeachment proceedings.

1869 First transcontinental railroad completed.

1869 Wyoming becomes first state to allow women to vote.

1871 Chicago leveled by fire.

1872 Yellowstone, the world's first National Park, set up.

1876 General George A. Custer defeated by Sioux Indians at the Little Big Horn River in Montana.

1879 F.W. Woolworth opens the first "five and dime" at Utica, New York.

1881 President James A. Garfield assassinated.

1886 Aftermath of Chicago's Haymarket Riots leads to formation of the American Federation of Labor.

1886 Statue of Liberty dedicated.

1890 Indian wars come to an end with the Battle of Wounded Knee in South Dakota.

1892 Ellis Island established as an immigration depot.

1894 Thomas A. Edison demonstrates moving pictures with his kinetoscope.

1898 U.S. goes to war with Spain for Cuban independence and wins Puerto Rico, the Philippines and Guam.

1898 U.S. annexes Hawaii.

1901 Oil gushes from the ground at Beaumont, Texas.

1903 Wilbur and Orville Wright fly their machine over the beach at Kitty Hawk, North Carolina.

1903 Treaty paves the way for digging the Panama Canal.

1906 San Francisco devastated by an earthquake and fire.

Facing page: *Statue of Liberty Dedication. New York, October 28, 1886.*

Above: *Custer's Last Stand. Little Big Horn, Montana, June 25, 1876.*

HISTORY OF AMERICA

1907	U.S. fleet sails around the world.
1909	Admiral Richard E. Peary reaches the North Pole.
1915	Alexander Graham Bell perfects the telephone.
1917	U.S. troops go to Europe after war declared on Germany.
1917	The Constitution's 18th Amendment, repealed in 1933, makes alcoholic beverages illegal.
1920	Commercial radio broadcasting begins.
1920	Constitutional Amendment gives women the vote.
1920	Arrest of 2,700 American Communists after "Red scare."
1921	Congress votes to put strong curbs on immigration.
1923	Lee de Forest demonstrates movies with sound.
1924	Congress grants citizenship to American Indians.
1927	Captain Charles A. Lindbergh flies solo from Long Island to Paris.
1929	Chicago gangsters celebrate Valentine's Day with a "rub out."
1929	Prosperity crashes on Wall Street.
1933	President Franklin Roosevelt begins "New Deal" programs to end the Great Depression.
1933	Prohibition of alcoholic beverages comes to an end.
1941	U.S. enters World War II after Japanese attack on Pearl Harbor in Hawaii.
1943	Income taxes first withheld from Americans' paychecks.
1945	First atomic bomb exploded at Alamogordo, New Mexico.
1945	Germany surrenders, May 7, and Japan capitulates, August 15, to end World War II.
1947	Secretary of State George C. Marshall, extends aid of some $12 billion to rebuild war-torn Europe.
1948	U.S. and Britain airlift supplies across Russian blockade of Berlin.
1950	American forces ordered to Korea to restore peace.
1951	Television goes intercontinental with first coast-to-coast broadcast.
1952	First hydrogen bomb exploded on Eniwetok Atoll in the South Pacific.
1954	Senator Joseph McCarthy condemned by U.S. Senate.
1954	U.S. launches *Nautilus*, the first nuclear-powered submarine.
1955	Supreme Court orders desegregation of schools.
1956	Interstate highway system inaugurated.
1957	Congress enacts civil rights legislation.
1958	U.S. launches its first orbiting satellite.
1958	First jet-powered airline service established between Miami and New York.
1959	Alaska and Hawaii become 49th and 50th states.
1959	St. Lawrence Seaway opens.
1960	Civil rights "sit-ins" begin in Greensboro, North Carolina.
1962	Astronaut John Glenn orbits the earth.
1962	U.S. announces its "advisors" in Vietnam will fire if fired upon.
1962	President Kennedy reveals presence of Soviet missiles in Cuba.
1963	President John F. Kennedy assassinated.
1964	Tonkin Resolution authorizes American participation in Vietnam War.
1966	U.S. forces carry Vietnam War into Cambodia.
1968	Rev. Dr. Martin Luther King, Jr. assassinated.

Above: *Edward F. Hinkle, an American pilot in the Lafayette Escadrille, Paris, France, June, 1917.*

1968   Senator Robert F. Kennedy assassinated.

1969   Neil A. Armstrong becomes first man on the moon.

1970   Students killed in anti-war demonstration, in Kent State, Ohio.

1970   Anti-pollution demonstrators celebrate first "Earth Day."

1971   Voting age reduced to 18.

1972   President Richard Nixon opens the door to Communist China.

1973   Supreme Court ruling overturns anti-abortion laws.

1973   Vice President Spiro T. Agnew resigns after tax-evasion charges.

1974   President Nixon resigns in wake of Watergate scandal.

1974   President Gerald R. Ford issues an unconditional pardon to former President Nixon.

1977   President Jimmy Carter issues a pardon to Vietnam War draft evaders.

1978   U.S. agrees to turn over Panama Canal to Panamanian control.

1979   Iranians storm embassy and take 63 American hostages.

1980   Beatle John Lennon is murdered in New York.

1981   Hostages released by Iran after 444 days of captivity.

1982   Space shuttle *Columbia* successfully launched and retrieved.

1982   After 13 years of legal battling, American Telephone and Telegraph gives up its telephone monopoly.

1982   Dr. Robert Jarvik demonstrates first successful artificial heart.

1983   A terrorist bomb kills 240 U.S. Marines in Lebanon.

1983   U.S. troops invade Caribbean island of Grenada.

1986   Government confirms an epidemic of AIDS.

1986   Government designates January 20 Martin Luther King Day.

1986   Space Shuttle *Challenger* explodes on liftoff.

1986   U.S. planes attack Libya and Tripoli.

1987   Iran-Contra scandal erupts.

1987   Federal budget first tops the trillion-dollar mark.

1987   Guided missile cruiser, U.S.S. *Stark*, sunk by Iraqi jet in the Persian Gulf.

1987   Stock market drops 22.6% in one day, worst decline since 1914.

1988   Four million acres of woodland, including much of Yellowstone National Park, destroyed in forest fires.

1989   Ruptured tanker *Exxon Valdez* spills 290,000 barrels of oil into Alaska's Prince William Sound.

1989   Supreme Court rules that flag burning is a legal form of political expression.

1989   Congress authorizes $300 billion to rescue the savings and loan industry.

1989   Severe earthquake rocks San Francisco/Oakland area.

1989   U.S. troops invade Panama and eventually take its President, Manuel Noriega, prisoner.

1991   U.S. forces join troops of 28 other nations to rescue Kuwait from Iraqi occupation.

1992   Acquittal of police officers involved in beating Rodney King leads to rioting in Los Angeles and death of 52.

1992   U.S. troops sent to Somalia to facilitate famine relief.

1993   U.S. and Russia agree to cut their nuclear arsenals to 3,500 and 3,000 warheads respectively, from the 12,477 and 11,320 held by each nation in 1989.

Top: *A National Organization for Women protest, Washington, D.C., May 7, 1969.*

Above: *Demonstrators outside the Democratic National Convention, Chicago, August 8, 1968.*

Overleaf: *An early 20th-century class of schoolchildren is taught something of the history and culture of Native Americans.*

PICTURE CREDITS

The publishers wish to thank the following individuals and organizations for granting permission to reproduce the illustrations used in this book:

BETTMANN ARCHIVE: endpapers, half-title page, title page, introduction page, 8-36, 41 (top), 42-108, 109 (top), 110-119, 121-143, 146-147 (bottom), 148-165, 167-189, 191, 192, 195, 196, 197 (left), 198, 200-203, 218-223;

MICHAEL OCHS ARCHIVES: contents page, 197 (right);

OLD STURBRIDGE VILLAGE/ROBERT S. ARNOLD: 37, 38-39, 40, 41 (bottom);

THE LIBRARY OF CONGRESS: 109 (bottom), 120, 166;

COLOUR LIBRARY BOOKS LTD.: 144-145, 146, 147 (top);

FPG INTERNATIONAL/L. WILLINGER: 190, 194 (top);

FPG INTERNATIONAL/R. BEATTIE: 194 (bottom);

SICKLES PHOTO-REPORTING: 193;

B. FRIEDMAN: 199, 205 (bottom left);

NEAL PETERS COLLECTION: 205 (top left);

ELLIOTT LANDY/RETNA: 205 (right);

GARY GERSHOFF/RETNA: 204;

DAVID TOERGE/BLACK STAR: 206;

DENNIS BRACK/BLACK STAR: 207, 211 (right);

FRED WARD/BLACK STAR: 208;

MANOOCHER/BLACK STAR: 209;

CINDY KARP/BLACK STAR: 210, 211 (left);

BOB KRIST/BLACK STAR: 212;

JAMES A. SUGAR/BLACK STAR: 213;

HIROYUKI MATSUMOTO/BLACK STAR: 214;

JIM STRATFORD/BLACK STAR: 215;

SHELLY KATZ/BLACK STAR: 216;

PAUL MILLER/BLACK STAR: 217.